MW01708087

Renoir

Phidal

“Man lives and dies in what he sees, but he sees only what he dreams”.

Paul Valéry

Pierre-Auguste Renoir was born in Limoges on February 25th, 1841. His father, Léonard Renoir, was a tailor by trade and his mother, Marguerite, a seamstress. Although the family belonged to the artisan middle-class and was never actually poor, they had to work hard for every penny they earned. In the hope of finding better working conditions, Léonard Renoir moved to Paris with his large family when Pierre-Auguste was just three. At the age of seven, he was sent to a school run by the Christian Brothers where he was taught reading, writing and arithmetic, as well as the rudiments of a musical education which revealed his gift for music. Since he also showed an early interest in drawing, his father took him away from the school in 1854 and apprenticed him to a firm of porcelain painters called Lévy Brothers. Here he began to paint flowers and Louis XVI decorations on porcelain plates, in keeping with the traditions of his native Limoges. He spent four years painting roses on plates and bouquets of flowers on teapots. He soon became skilful at this, and his employers began to entrust him with more and more difficult assignments.

In the evenings he attended classes at the School of Design and Decorative Arts in Rue des Petits-Carreaux. Here he made the acquaintance of the painter Emile Laporte who persuaded him, without much difficulty, to take up painting.

In 1858, the year of the start of the Second Republic and a time of great social change, the Lévy Brothers were forced to close down: industrialized methods were coming into use and in the porcelain business the machine was taking over the craftsman.

Renoir went to work for M. Gilbert, a painter of religious subjects for missionaries. He painted the Virgin and Child and pictures of Saints on canvas strips which the missionaries would unroll and hang up in their makeshift churches, and managed to earn quite a good living. Soon he had quite a few savings put by and decided that the time had come to fulfil one of his dreams: he applied for admission to the Ecole des Beaux-Arts and passed the entrance examination for the summer session of 1862, coming 68th out of 80. He enrolled in the studios of Emile Signol and Marc-Charles-Gabriel Gleyre. Although his teachers at the Ecole des Beaux-Arts hardly noticed him, he nevertheless made the acquaintance of other young artists such as Claude Monet, Frédéric

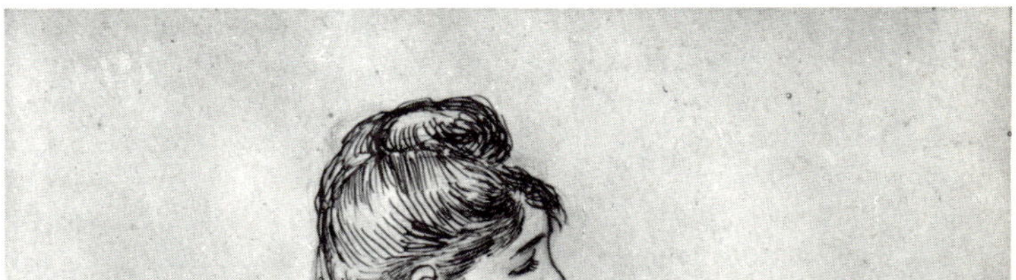

Bather, Musée du Louvre, Paris.

Bazille, and the Englishman Alfred Sisley with whom he struck up a close friendship.
At that time the art world was in turmoil. In 1863 Manet had painted *Déjeuner sur l'herbe* and in 1865 *Olympia*, and Renoir and his friends grouped around him to take part in the renaissance of French painting now known as Impressionism, a name invented almost in jest when, in 1874, Monet presented his painting *Impression: Sunrise* at the Exhibition of Independent Artists held in April in the studio of the photographer Nadar.
Renoir soon realized that his views on art were very different from those of his teachers, so in 1863 he left the Ecole des Beaux-Arts, taking his friends with him, and went to paint in the open air in the Forest of Fontainebleau. Here he met Courbet, who had a great influence on his work, and also Diaz who one day said to him, "no painter with self-respect will ever pick up a brush unless he has his model right in front of him". According to Edouard, Renoir's brother, these words "always remained engraved upon his memory".
Until the Franco-Prussian War of 1870, Renoir, with his haversack on his back, was a frequent visitor to the Forest of Fontainebleau, taking board and lodging either with Père Paillard at the Auberge du Cheval-Blanc in Chailly-en-Bière or with Mère Anthony at Marlotte, or enjoying the generous hospitality of his friend and fellow painter, Jules Le Coeur.
In the home of Jules Le Coeur, Renoir met Lise Tréhot, the younger sister of Le Coeur's charming mistress Clémence. Lise soon became his favourite model and over the next few years he painted over twenty portraits of her: *Diana* and *Woman with a Sunshade* in 1867, *The Gypsy Girl* in 1868, and *Odalisque, or Woman of Algiers* in 1870, a large canvas worthy of Delacroix, where Lise is portrayed wearing extravagant Oriental clothes. In 1872 Renoir painted his last portrait of Lise looking tenderly at a parakeet perched on her hand in front of an open cage. On April 24th, 1872 Lise married the young architect Georges Brière de l'Isle, and from then on she devoted herself to her family. She never again saw the great artist whose favourite model she had been.
In his first portraits of Lise, Renoir still used a traditional technique, with a fairly dark colour scheme, smoothly blended paints and scumblings which allowed the priming coats to show through. In *Woman with a Sunshade* and *The Gypsy Girl*, however, he used more modern means that heralded the technique of *Le Moulin de la Galette*: his subject was sketched directly onto the unprimed canvas, he used ochre and vermilion and replaced the earth colours of his earlier portraits with blues. By now he was an advocate of bright colours which he regarded as more suitable for rendering the effects of light and the open air.
During this period he shared Sisley's studio at Porte Maillot and when Sisley got married, he moved to the house of Frédéric Bazille, first in Rue Visconti and then at no. 9, Rue de la Condamine in the Batignolles district. Here he painted a charming portrait of his host. Bazille is shown sitting in front of his easel wearing red slippers, his elbows on his knees, staring at the still life he is painting.
At Bazille's house he also met Edmond Maître, the dilettante from Bordeaux who introduced him to various other artists and writers. With Maître he often went to the Café Guerbois in the Grand-Rue des Batignolles to meet Edouard Manet, and his old friends from the Beaux-Arts, or the novelist Emile Zola and his childhood friend Paul Cézanne.
Then war broke out. In 1870 Napoleon III declared war on Prussia. The Prussian invasion took Renoir by surprise at a time when he was engrossed in his work, but he immediately enlisted in the 10th Cavalry Regiment. On August 10th Bazille joined the 3rd Regiment of Zouaves. Garrisoned first at Tarbes, Renoir was then sent to Libourne where he became seriously ill. He was released from service in 1871 and immediately returned to Paris. The disaster suffered by the French at Sedan on September 2nd led to the fall of the Second Empire and the proclamation of the 3rd Republic. The siege of Paris deprived Renoir of news about his friends: Monet and Pissarro had gone to England and Bazille died in November 1871, though Renoir learnt the news only a long time afterwards. In January 1872, still feeling isolated in Paris, Renoir met Paul Durand-Ruel, a dealer at the Rue Laffitte gallery who bought his *Pont des Arts and the Institute* for 200 francs. By showing confidence in them in this way, Durand-Ruel associated his own career with that of the Impressionists, whose efforts he supported until they finally achieved recognition and fame. At this time, Renoir was finishing his large composition *Parisian Women Dressed as Algerians* which he exhibited without success in the Salon of 1872 and which includes, for the last time, the sober, lovely features of Lise Tréhot. In September 1873 Renoir rented an attic at no. 35, Rue Saint-Georges in Montmartre. Here he started two paintings which were to become famous: *The Loge*, showing a couple in a box at the theatre, and *The Dancer*. He presented them from April 15th to May 15th 1874 at the first group exhibition of the Impressionists (who at that time called themselves Société Anonyme Coopérative des Artistes Peintres, Sculpteurs, Graveurs), held as an alternative to the official Salon in the Paris gallery of the photographer Nadar at 35, Boulevard des Capucines.
Unfortunately the exhibition was not a success. "The public flocked to it", related Paul Durand-Ruel in his memoirs, "but with an obvious bias, and saw in these great artists nothing but ignorant and presumptuous men trying to attract attention by their eccentricities. Public opinion then turned against them, and a general outburst of hilarity, scorn, and even indignation spread through all circles of society - the studios, salons, even the theatres, where they were held up to ridicule." Nevertheless, Renoir managed to sell *The Loge* to a dealer, Père Martin, for 425 francs.
The independent painters often used to meet at the Café La Nouvelle Athènes in the Place Pigalle. There Renoir met his friends and also young painters such as Franc-Lamy, Norbert Goetneutte and Frédéric Cordey, as well as an employee of the Ministry of Finance, Georges Rivière, who was to become his biographer. In the hope of solving their financial difficulties, Renoir, Monet, Sisley and Berthe Morisot decided to organize a public sale of Impressionist paintings. It took place on March 24th, 1875 at the Hôtel Drouot but unfortunately was a complete fiasco. Albert Wolff, writing in *Le Figaro*, called them "monkeys with paintbrushes in their hands" and the twenty canvases Renoir had put up for sale brought in only the miserable sum of 2,251 francs. The sale did however have one happy result for Renoir. It was there that he made the acquaintance of Victor Chocquet, a Customs official, who was to become one of the artist's strongest supporters. Renoir painted several portraits of Chocquet's family and also sold him many other pictures.
In April 1875 Renoir was paid 1,200 francs for his painting called *La Promenade* and was able to rent two attic rooms at 12, Rue Cortot in Montmartre and an old stable on the ground floor of the same 17th century building, which he used as a studio. Behind the stable there was a peaceful garden where Renoir painted several portraits of the actress Henriette Henriot, the young model Nini Lopez, and Claude Monet.
In spring 1876, on the premises of the Moulin de la Galette, he sketched out several large canvases: *The Arbour*, *Nude in the Sun*, *The Swing*, and the famous *Le Moulin de la Galette*.
On the top of the Butte Montmartre, adjoining Rue Lepic, amidst the gardens and fields of Montmartre as it was then, there was a large, square shed between two old windmills, with a platform for an orchestra and a large, shaded garden. This was the Moulin de la Galette dance hall, managed by Messrs. Debray father and son, where the people of Montmartre came to dance on Sunday afternoons and holidays. Renoir

had formed a plan to paint a large composition showing this popular spot and the result was a radiant canvas summing up the atmosphere of a whole period: it was quickly bought by Renoir's friend and fellow painter Gustave Caillebotte.
When shown at the third group exhibition of the Impressionists, *Le Moulin de la Galette* was warmly praised by Georges Rivière in the first issue of *L'Impressionniste* (Paris, 1877): "It is a page of history, a precious and strictly accurate memento of Parisian life..... Its boldness is bound to have the success it deserves."
During this period Renoir applied himself to a poetic rendering of light effects, both in his nudes and in his open-air figure groups.
He had long continued to mix his colours on the palette and work with scumblings, following the technique used in *The Loge* or *The Dancer*. From 1876 on, however, he made use of a new technique which, by boldly applying optical laws, he juxtaposed on the canvas tiny dabs of different colours which then merge in the spectator's eye while retaining their vibrant qualities.
In September 1876, after finishing *Le Moulin de la Galette*, Renoir stayed for three weeks on the edge of the Forest of Champrosay in the home of the novelist Alphonse Daudet, where he had the pleasure of painting a portrait of Daudet's young wife. On his return to Paris, his financial situation improved as a result of his meeting with the publisher Georges Charpentier, who had purchased Renoir's *Angler* at the sale held on March 27th 1875, and now wished to meet the artist who had painted it.
Renoir soon became a regular guest at the receptions of Madame Charpentier where he met politicians like Gambetta and Jules Ferry, the writer Emile Zola who had just published *L'Assommoir* in serial form, Edmond de Goncourt, and Théodore de Banville. The Charpentiers commissioned Renoir to paint a portrait of their children, Paul and Georgette, and then one of Madame Charpentier with her son, her daughter, and their dog Porto in the Japanese room of the family's townhouse at 11, Rue de Grenelle. Thanks to the influence and connections of the publisher, this painting was exhibited at the Salon where it was a great success.
In February 1880, at Mme. Camille's dairy where he often took his meals, Renoir met a young milliner called Aline Charigot who was just twenty. Since the painter's studio was close to the apartment where Aline lived with her mother, Aline often came to pose for Renoir and soon the friendship ripened into love. On Sundays they often went together to La Grenouillère or to Chatou, near the Pont de Croissy, to the inn of Père Fournaise whose daughter, Alphonsine, had been the subject of a charming portrait by Renoir the previous year. Using the same setting, Renoir now planned a large canvas of a boating party. He had already painted Aline wearing a red dress in a picture with other boaters, and now he sketched *The Luncheon of the Boating Party*, representing the end of a convivial meal: in the left foreground is Aline wearing a flowery hat and stretching her head towards her Pekingese dog; further back we can see Alphonsine Fournaise leaning against the railings, and in the background stands Paul Lhote. Renoir finished the painting in his studio during the winter of 1880-1881.
In a moment of moral and artistic crisis and wishing to "renew his vision", in February 1881, Renoir suddenly decided to leave for Algeria. He was accompanied by Corday, and Lestringuez and Paul Lhote were to join them later. On March 4th Renoir wrote to Théodore Duret: "I wanted to see what the land of the sun was like. I am out of luck for there is scarcely any at the moment. But it is exquisite all the same, an extraordinary wealth of nature." He stayed in Algiers about a month and returned the following year.
During his stays he painted *Grove of Banana Trees*, *Ali*, and *The Ravine of the Wild Woman*, as well as some studies of Arab types in the Casbah and a few sketches of landscapes.
In between his visits to Algeria he went to Italy: he did not like Milan or Padua, but Venice thrilled him with its vibrant colours. He painted a picture of St. Mark's and one of some gondoliers on the Grand Canal, with warm colours. At the Palazzo Pitti in Florence he saw Raphael's *Madonna della Sedia* and then went to Rome "to see the Raphaels" in the Vatican Stanze, the real reason for his visit to Italy. To Durand-Ruel he wrote: "They are truly fine and I should have seen them sooner. They are full of learning and wisdom. Unlike me he was not looking for impossible things, but it is very beautiful." In December, Pompeii increased his artistic excitement and stimulated him to research further: "I am like a schoolchild who has a white sheet of paper in front of him on which he must try to write neatly. Then, bang! A blot of ink. I am still struggling with these blots and I am forty years old". After visiting Naples he stopped off at Capri just long enough to paint *The Blond Bather*, a nude of a young woman bathed in the light of the sun. Then he moved on to Sicily.
His friend M. Lascoux, a great music lover, had commissioned him to paint a portrait of Richard Wagner who was putting the finishing touches to *Parsifal* in Palermo. In thirty-five minutes Renoir painted the great composer who, in front of the still-wet canvas, exclaimed: "Ah! Ah! I look like a Protestant Minister!".
After a stay at L'Estaque, where he met Cézanne again, Renoir returned to Paris where the patient Aline was awaiting him: in the spring of 1882 they finally decided to set up house together.
The journey to Italy left its mark on Renoir. The murals at Pompeii and the archaeological treasures revealed to him the art of the ancients and he was disturbed by his discoveries. He studied drawing eagerly and became obsessed with the search for form.
Nymphs Bathing, a lead bas-relief by Girardon, which adorns the Allée des Marmousets in the gardens at Versailles, drew his attention and provided him with the subject of the large composition he had been thinking about ever since his return from Italy. The painting would depict a group of playful woman bathers, some sitting on the riverbank, others standing in the water.
His savings, however, were being used up and so, for the moment, he had to return to well-paid portrait painting. He painted the five children of Durand-Ruel and for the same dealer did a second version of the *The Blond Bather*, which Durand-Ruel soon sold to Paul Gallimard. He also sketched two large figure compositions on the theme of dancing which marked the beginning of what he called his "harsh manner" or Ingresque period. His manner of painting was in fact changing. As he himself wrote to Ambroise Vollard: "About 1883, a kind of break occurred in my work. I had got to the very end with Impressionism and came to the realization that I didn't know how to paint or draw. In a word, I had come to a deadlock."
In the meantime *The Large Bathers* was slowly taking shape. Renoir made numerous preparatory studies in pencil and red chalk, as well as several oil sketches. On January 1st 1886, Berthe Morisot visited her friend's studio and wrote the following in her notebook: "It would be interesting to show all these preparatory studies to a public which generally assumes that the Impressionists work at top speed. I do not believe that one could go any further in rendering form in a drawing. These nude women going into the sea delight me quite as much as those of Ingres. Renoir tells me that the nude for him is one of the most indispensable forms of art." The open air no longer attracted him since too much light had a harmful effect on the form and the design; what he sought after now was style, lines, composition, the structure of things, volumes and space. With Monet, he burnt some of the paintings they had done during their previous period and from now on Renoir painted only in the artificial light of his studio. "Outdoors," he wrote to Ambroise Vollard, "you have a greater variety of light than with studio lighting, which is always the same. But outside, for that very reason, you

are so taken up by the light that you don't have time to pay enough attention to composition and so you don't really see what you are doing".

In 1887 he completed *The Large Bathers*.

In 1884, when Aline was expecting their first child, Renoir went to look for a new studio and a new apartment: the former was at 37, Rue Laval (now Rue Victor Massé) and the latter at 18, Rue Houdon where, on March 21st, 1885, the artist's eldest son, Pierre, was born. From then on, Renoir devoted himself entirely to family life and his favourite models became his wife and his children. Jean Renoir has described this period well in a book he wrote about his father: "More important than theories, I think, was Renoir's transition from bachelorhood to being a married man. Restless, incapable of staying in one place, he would suddenly jump on a train with the vague hope of enjoying the soft light of Guernesey or losing himself in the pink reflections of Blida. Since leaving the Rue des Gravilliers he had forgotten the meaning of the word 'home'. Now, all at once, he found himself in an apartment with a wife: meals at regular hours, a neatly made bed, and his socks mended. And to all these blessings was soon to be added that of a child. The arrival of my brother Pierre was to work the great revolution in Renoir's life. The theories heard at the Nouvelle Athènes were superseded by a dimple on a newborn baby's thigh".

Between 1885 and 1886 Renoir painted various versions of motherhood, all intense and full of charm, to confirm the new orientation of his art.

Mother and child are the subject of numerous paintings, pastels, red chalk, pencil and pen and ink drawings, and Renoir was so fond of the theme that thirty years later, in 1916, he asked the sculptor Richard Guino to execute for him a piece of sculpture showing Aline, with a straw hat on her head, nursing her infant Pierre in the garden of Essoyes.

In April 1888 Renoir painted the three daughters of the poet Catulle Mendès grouped around the piano: the portrait was commissioned, though grossly underpaid. Fortunately, however, Renoir was now able to count on purchases made by new dealers interested in his work. In addition to Durand-Ruel, now absorbed in setting up a business in the United States, there were also Georges Petit, Boussod, Valladon and the influential firm of Knoedler.

During the summer of 1888 he stayed for a time on the banks of the Seine at Argenteuil, Bougival, or Petit-Genevilliers with his friend Caillebotte. Here he painted nudes, bathers, *Little Girl with Sheaf of Grass and Wildflowers* and three variations on the same theme of *Young Girl Carrying a Basket of Flowers*. *La Coiffure*, one of his "harsh" compositions showing a young girl arranging her hair after bathing, can also be dated to the same period.

In 1889, to celebrate the centenary of the French Revolution, the World Exhibition opened in Paris and at the Champ-de-Mars, Eiffel built the tower that bears his name. For Renoir, the same year corresponds to the start of his "iridescent" period. His previous "Ingresque" period had been precise and linear but now he broke away and while still retaining his incomparable sense of volume and full-bodied forms, he regained the freedom of his youth.

During a short stay at Essoyes, his wife's native town, he painted several versions of *The Apple Vendor*. He took advantage of the hospitality of Berthe Morisot, who with her husband Eugène Manet, Edouard's brother, had rented a house in Mézy, near Meulan. With the added benefit of Berthe's charming models, he painted *Two Girls Picking Flowers* and *In the Meadow, or Gathering Flowers*. He went no further with these themes, however, and from 1890 onwards he devoted himself almost exclusively to nudes and portraits. With whites and pinks and half-tints that give the compositions a pearly sheen, in 1890 he painted *Little Girls with a Charlotte Hat* and *Two Sisters Reading*; these were followed in 1892 by *Bather Sitting on a Rock* and in 1894 by *Girls by the Seaside* and variations on the theme of *At the Piano*.

In about 1890, at the height of his artistic career, Renoir was stricken with rheumatism, a cruel disease that gave him no respite. Hoping to find some relief from his pain he decided to move to the south of France and in 1903, after staying for a short while in Magagnosc and Le Cannet, he settled in Cagnes where he rented a spacious apartment in the Maison de la Poste.

From his windows he had a fine view of the town and its surroundings, bathed in the sunlight of Provence with the warm colours set off by the nearness of the sea. Despite the wonders of nature that surrounded him, however, Renoir's favourite subjects remained his wife and his sons: Pierre, Jean - the future film director born on September 15th, 1894 - and little Claude, nicknamed "Coco", born on August 1st, 1901 when his father was in his sixtieth year. There was also Gabrielle, the young peasant girl from Essoyes, whom Renoir had hired as a maid to help Aline when Jean was born and who had remained part of the family ever since.

From 1907 to 1910 Renoir painted numerous portraits of Gabrielle and she remained his favourite model for years. *Gabrielle with Bare Breasts* is dated 1907 and *Gabrielle before a Mirror with Jewellery* 1910. The paintings represent the outcome of Renoir's experiments in figure painting.

Sometimes Renoir liked to go out in an old victoria driven by Baptistin to a place called Les Collettes, not far from Cagnes. Here there were giant olive trees and a splendid view across the sea to the Cap d'Antibes or even further as far as the Estérel range. On June 28th, 1907, six years after his move to the south of France, Renoir became the owner of Les Collettes and its two and a half hectares of olive trees, medlars, orange trees, and a small vineyard. Since there was only an old farmhouse on the land, Renoir had a large stone house built with a studio upstairs. The olive garden soon became an unfailing source of fresh inspiration. At the same time Renoir began to study Classical Antiquity. "What admirable creatures those Greeks were!" he said one day to the poet Gasquet. "They lived so happy a life that they imagined the gods came down to earth in order to find their paradise and true love. Yes, the earth was the paradise of the gods .... And that is what I wish to paint".

In 1908 he painted the first version of the *Judgement of Paris*, followed by two large oil sketches for *The Rhône and the Saône*.

At the end of June 1914 the assassination of the Austrian Archduke Franz Ferdinand led to the outbreak of war. France called up its men in August: Pierre joined the 4th Infantry Regiment and Jean was Artillery Sergeant in the 1st Regiment of Dragoons.

With two of his sons at the front, Renoir's thoughts were only for them. After weeks of anxiety, waiting in vain day after day for news, Renoir finally learned that both his sons had been seriously wounded. Pierre had fought in Lorraine and had been sent to the Hospital of Carcassonne while Jean was recovering at Gérardner. Although it was a relief to learn that they were still alive, Renoir and his wife were extremely worried about their state of health. Aline rushed off to see them but she returned home exhausted and distressed by the horrors of war. On her arrival at Cagnes she took to bed and never recovered. Renoir had her sent to a hospital in Nice, where she died on June 28th, 1915. Renoir survived her by only a few years.

In August 1919, after a stay at Essoyes, he spent several weeks in Paris where he had the pleasure of seeing his *Portrait of Madame Charpentier* exhibited in the Louvre: it had been bought by the State and was on display in the La Caze exhibition hall.

This was one of his final pleasures.

He died at Cagnes on December 3rd, 1919, at two o'clock in the morning. A small still life of two apples remained unfinished on his drawing-board.

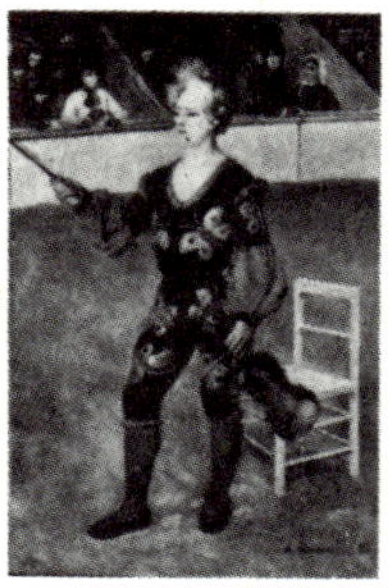

1. The Clown – 1868. Rijksmuseum Kröller-Müller, Otterlo – *The world of the circus fascinated French artists of the second half of the nineteenth century, opposed as they were to the representation of the traditional themes of academic painting. In this 1868 canvas, Renoir painted the world of the circus which was a great source of attraction for the young Impressionists.*

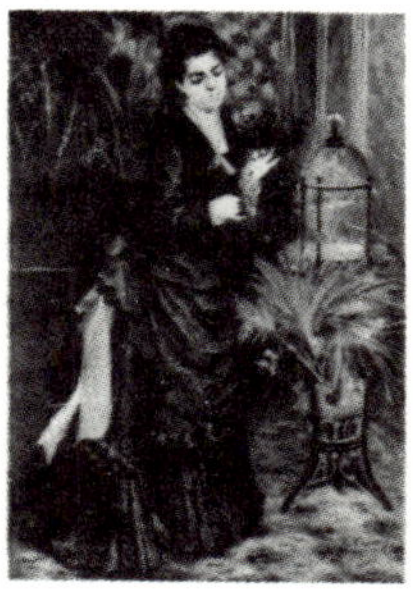

2. Lady with a Parakeet – 1871. Solomon R. Guggenheim Foundation (Tannhauser Collection), New York – *This was the last portrait of Lise Tréhot painted by Renoir just before her marriage. It was also one of the first pictures painted by Renoir on his return to Paris after the Franco-Prussian War.*

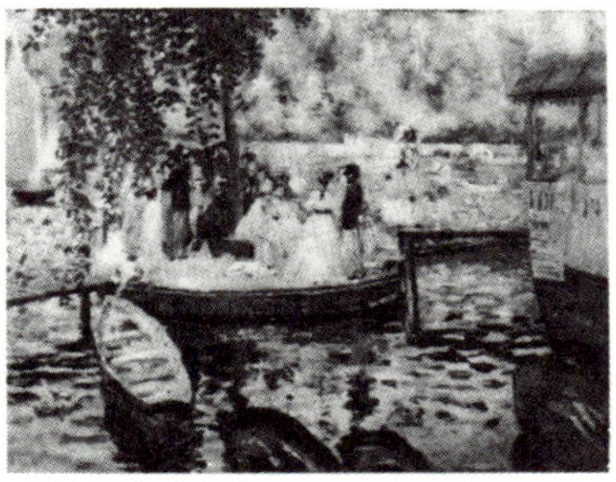

3. La Grenouillère – 1869. National Museum, Stockholm – *Radiant light, silhouettes, and objects reflected in the water, giving the impression of a moment of happiness and peace; the small, thick dabs of paint give an excellent impression of the patches of light on the sparkling water.*

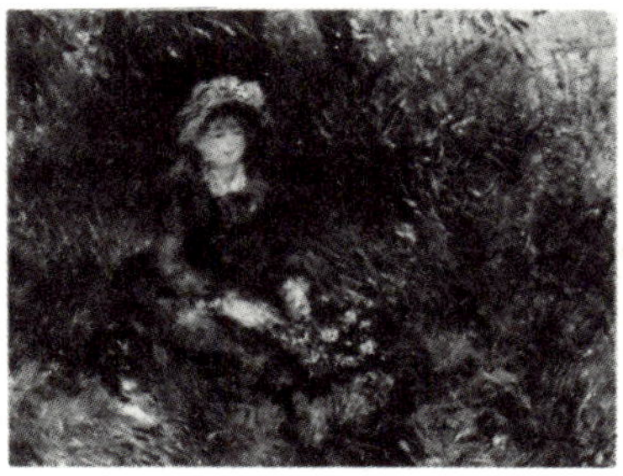

4. Madame Renoir with her Dog – 1880. Private collection, Paris – *Even when Renoir adopts the Impressionist style completely, the colours and the definition of his portraits are clear and never blurred like the landscapes. The young woman in this portrait is Aline Charigot, soon to become Renoir's wife.*

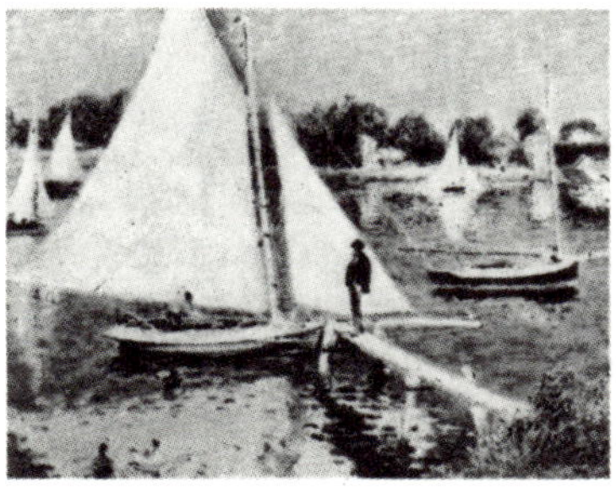

5. The Seine at Argenteuil – 1873-74. Portland Museum of Art, Oregon – *Like* La Grenouillère, *this picture was painted by Renoir when in the company of Monet. In these years of enthusiastic innovation, the Impressionists often met at Argenteuil where they loved the boats and the happy atmosphere of people enjoying themselves.*

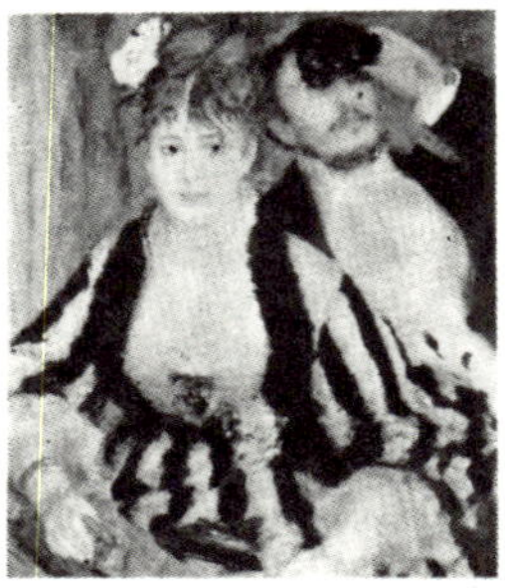

6. The Loge – 1874. Courtauld Institute Galleries, London – *This is one of Renoir's most famous paintings, presented at the First Impressionist Exhibition held in 1874 in the studio of the photographer Nadar. The subject, the search for form, and the luminous outlines make this an excellent example of impressionist art.*

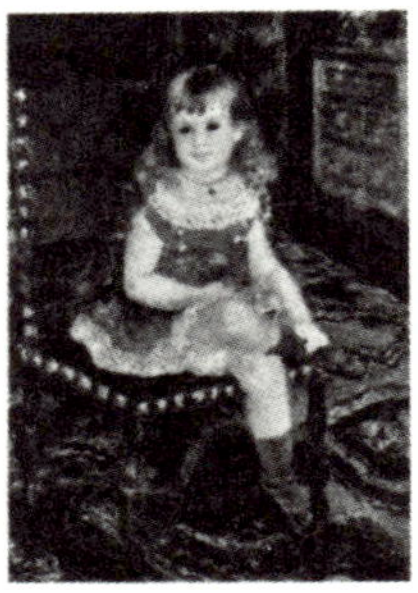

7. Mademoiselle Georgette Charpentier Seated – 1876. Private collection, New York – *This painting dates back to 1876 when Renoir became a close friend of the publisher Georges Charpentier and was often invited to his house. The charm and freshness the artist manages to impart to the portraits of the publisher's children demonstrate his sensitivity to childhood innocence.*

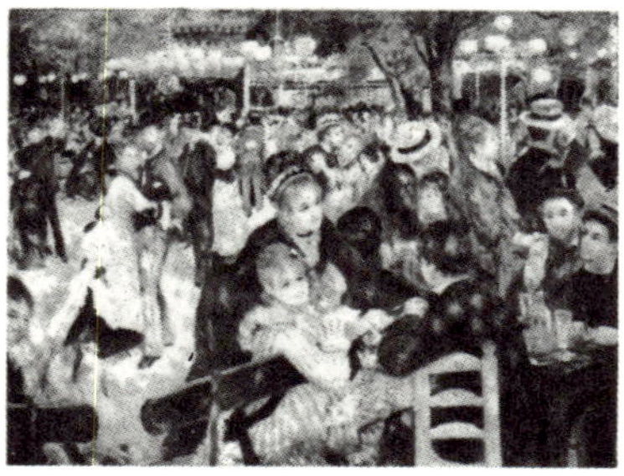

8. Le Moulin de la Galette – 1876. Musée d'Orsay, Paris – *Renoir loved the sincerity and gaiety of this Parisian open-air dance hall. In this radiant canvas, dancing couples whirl over the floor in the iridescent light of a summer afternoon. A festive atmosphere full of colour and merriment.*

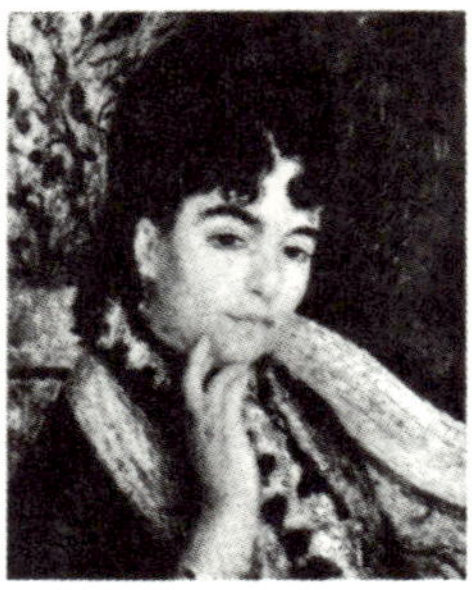

9. Portrait of Madame Alphonse Daudet – 1876. Musée du Louvre, Paris – *At Madame Charpentier's receptions, which at the time were the most important of their kind in Paris, Renoir made the acquaintance of many of the leading figures in the city's cultural life. He was often hired as their official portrait painter and always accepted willingly since such contacts enabled him to take part in interesting discussions and debates.*

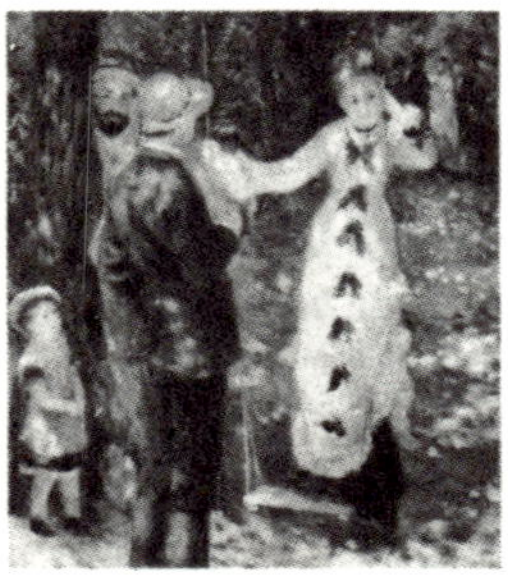

10. The Swing – 1876. Musée du Louvre, Paris – *During this period Renoir had rented a studio in rue Cortot in Montmartre with a large garden at the back where his friends often came to visit him. This canvas, painted during the same period and with the same technique as* Le Moulin de la Galette, *captures the simple, friendly atmosphere of these visits.*

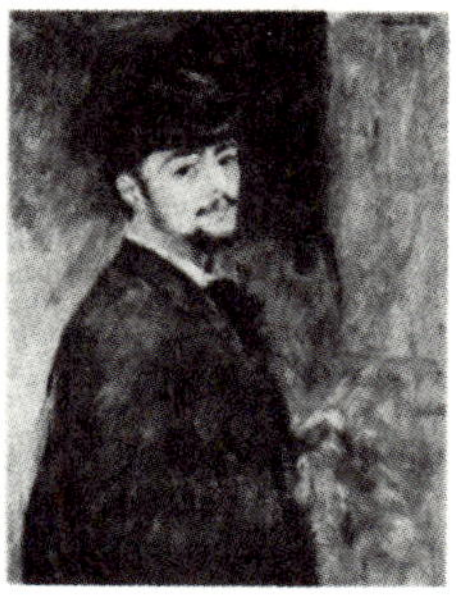

11. Self-Portrait – 1876. Fogg Art Museum, Cambridge (Mass.). By courtesy of Harvard University, Maurice Wertheim Collection – *The delicate plasticity with which Renoir portrayed his models can also be seen in this self-portrait of 1876, where the face is represented with care while the silhouette and the background are slightly blurred.*

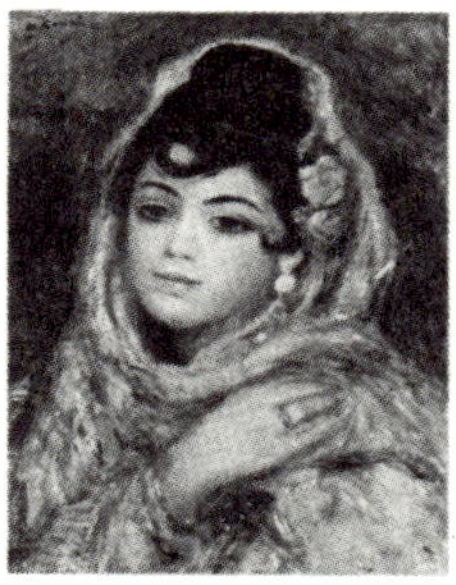

12. Algerian Woman – 1881. Solomon R. Guggenheim Foundation (Tannhauser Collection), New York – *In 1881 Renoir went to Algeria with his friend and fellow painter Corday to see the country which had been such a source of inspiration for Delacroix. In Algeria, he painted numerous landscapes and several portraits of Algerian women, such as the simple, charming one shown here.*

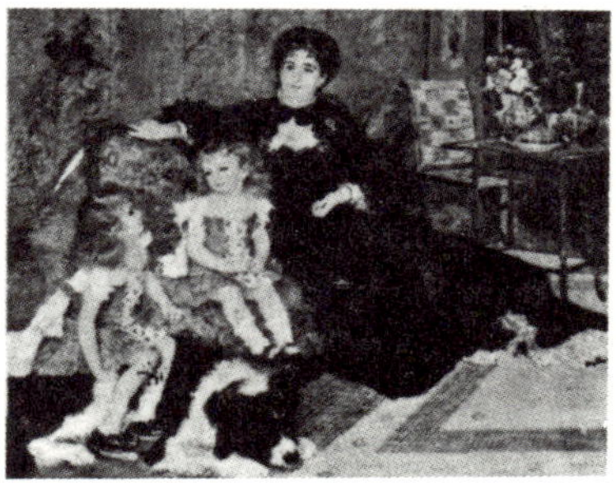

13. Madame Georges Charpentier and Her Daughters – 1878. Metropolitan Museum of Art (Wolfe Fund), New York – *This famous large composition, which Renoir painted in 1878, turned out to be a keypoint in his career: it was exhibited at the Salon in 1879 and was unanimously acclaimed by critics for the charm and freshness the artist had given to his characters and to the period environment.*

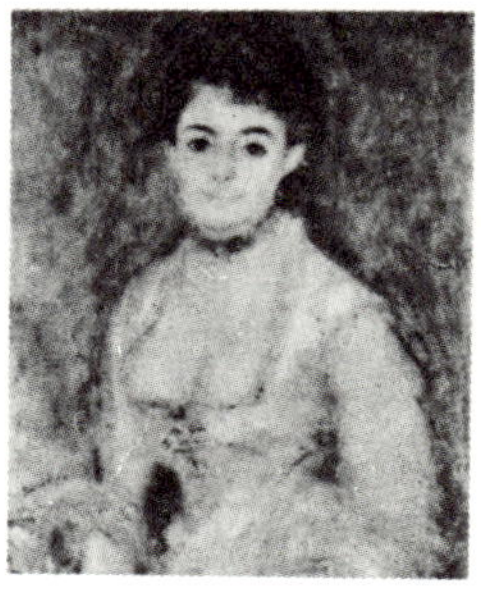

14. Portrait of Madame Henriot – c. 1877. National Gallery of Art (Gift of Adèle R. Levy Fund Inc.), Washington, D.C. – *The lady on the canvas is bathed in shimmering light and airy colours and the painting has a hazy, well-blended effect. It is a characteristic example of the results Renoir managed to achieve.*

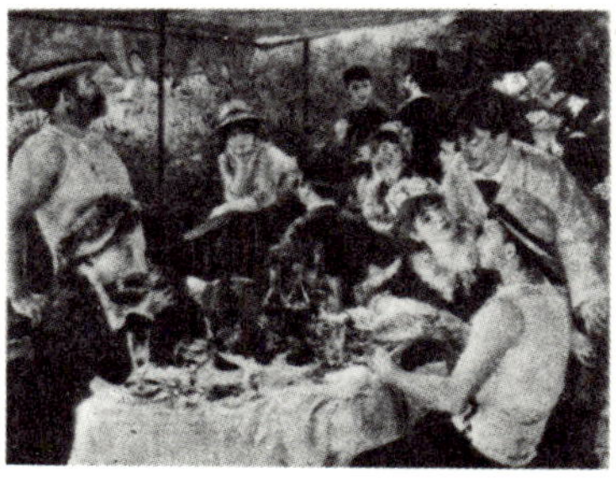

15. The Luncheon of the Boating Party – 1880-1881. Phillips Collection, Washington, D.C. – *This large composition, started in 1880 and completed in 1881, was Renoir's tribute to his own world. In a restaurant on the banks of the Seine, in the summer sunshine, Renoir depicts his friends in their everyday attitudes with a richness and detail worthy of the artists of the Renaissance.*

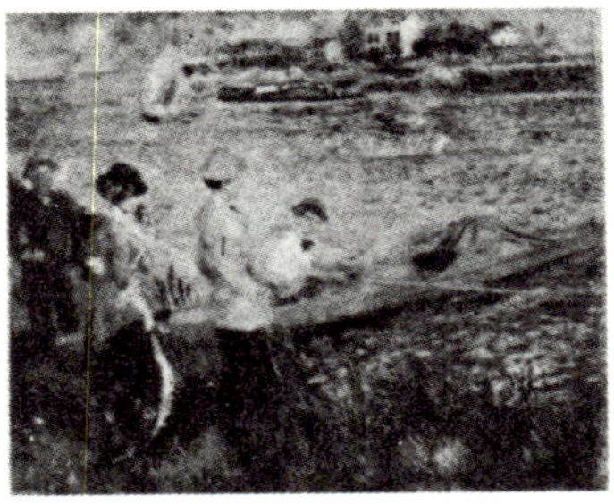

16. Boating Party at Chatou – 1879. National Gallery of Art, Washington, D.C. – *Now a master of the impressionist technique, in this 1879 canvas, Renoir painted one of his favourite pastimes on the banks of the Seine. Small, rapid brushstrokes convey the mirror effect of the water and the natural light which become part of the atmosphere created by the landscape and the figures.*

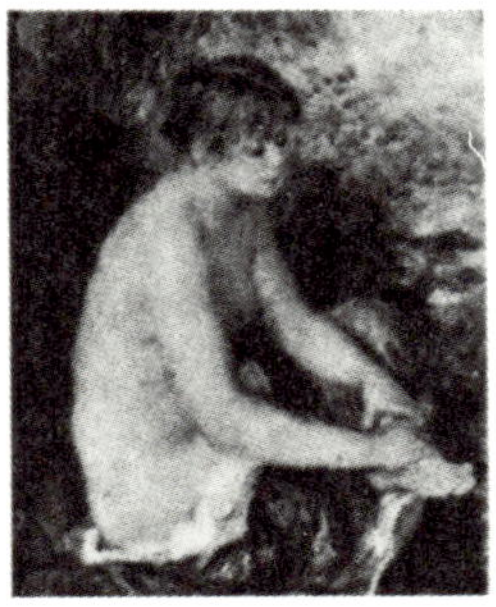

17. Little Blue Nude – 1879. The Albright-Knox Art Gallery, Buffalo (N.Y.) – *Renoir believed that the female nude was the most indispensable form of art since, as he himself wrote, "it is impossible to imagine anything more beautiful". This painting, dated 1879, emphasizes the grace of the silhouette while at the same time attenuating the outlines and the background by means of warmer colours.*

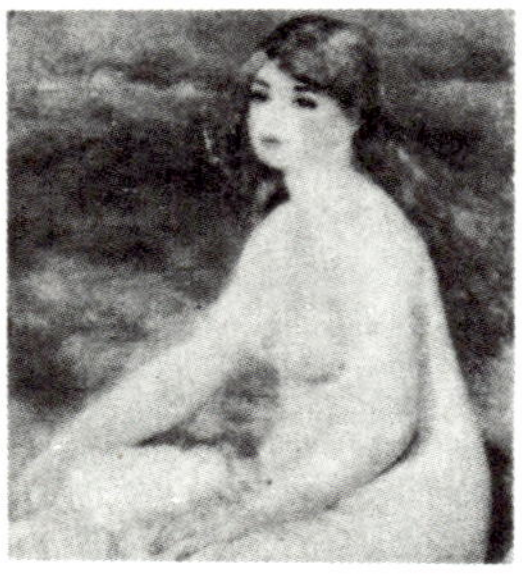

18. The Blond Bather – 1881-1882. Private collection, Turin - *During his stay in Italy where he had gone "to see the Raphaels" and the Pompeii murals, Renoir underwent new experiences which contributed to the vigorous plastic construction of this nude of a bather, painted in Naples.*

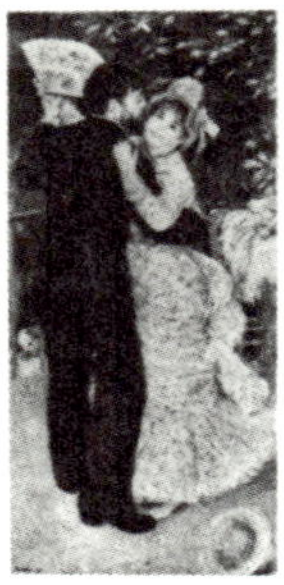

19. Dancing in the Country – 1883. Musée d'Orsay, Paris – *At the end of 1882 the art dealer Paul Durand-Ruel commissioned Renoir to paint three pictures of the same size on the theme of dancing. Renoir used his future wife, Aline Charigot, as his model, together with his friend and fellow painter Paul Lhote.*

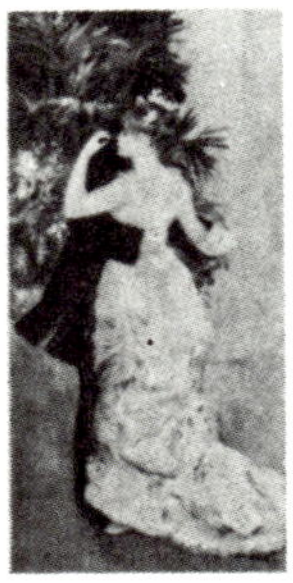

20. Dancing in Town – 1883. Musée d'Orsay, Paris – *In this second painting, as in the first, the portrait of the woman predominates: her personality is accurately portrayed whereas the man remains anonymous. Renoir highlights the delicate profile of the young woman and the luminosity of her dress.*

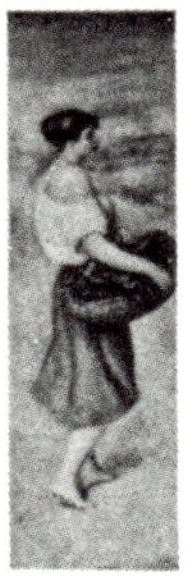

21. The Fish Vendor – c. 1889. National Gallery of Art, Washington, D.C. – *This female figure, bathed in sunlight and painted in delicate outline, blends perfectly with the background. The colours merge to envelop the figure in a warm, golden glow.*

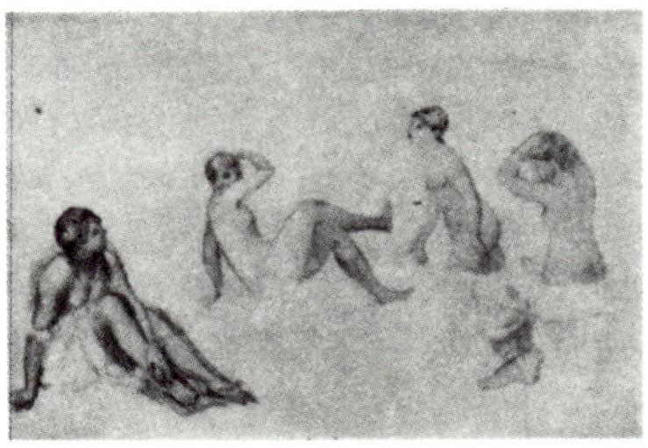

22. Sketch for "The Large Bathers" – 1884-1885. M. Paul Pétridès Collection, Paris – *This is one of the many studies, two of which were done in oils, which Renoir made between 1883 and 1886 in preparation for a large composition showing a group of bathers, which he had had in mind ever since his return from Italy in 1882.*

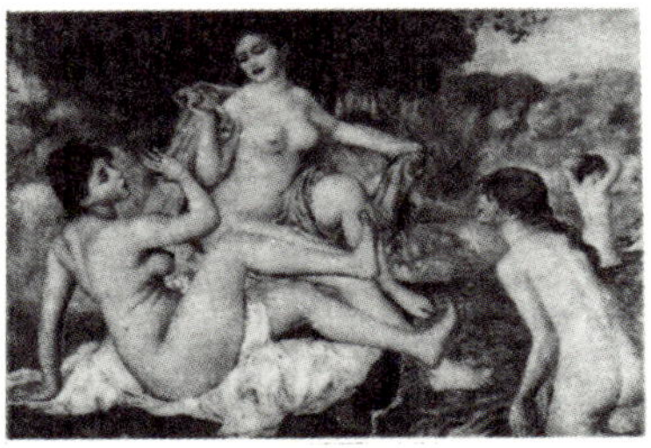

23. The Large Bathers – 1887. Mrs.C.S. Tyson Collection, Philadelphia – *Renoir worked for three years on this important work. The quest for form and design makes the outlines linear and precise. The deliberate style gives the painting a decorative appeal without excluding the sensation of gaiety.*

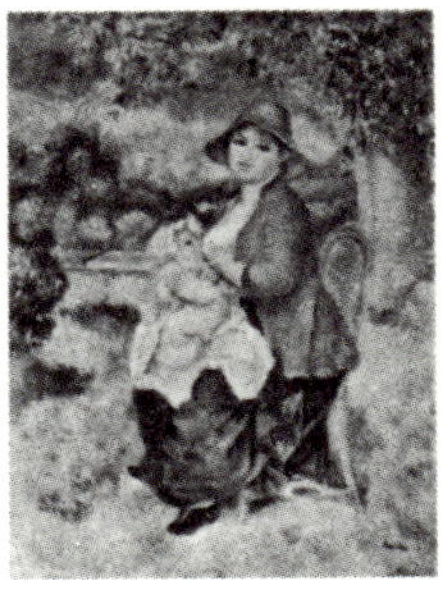

24. Motherhood, or Woman Nursing Her Child – 1886. Private collection, New York – *In this 1886 canvas, which shows Renoir's wife nursing their first child, the artist's reaction to the risk of allowing the forms to dissolve into Impressionist style has led to a vivid contrast between the precise, well-defined outlines of the portrait and the typically impressionist background.*

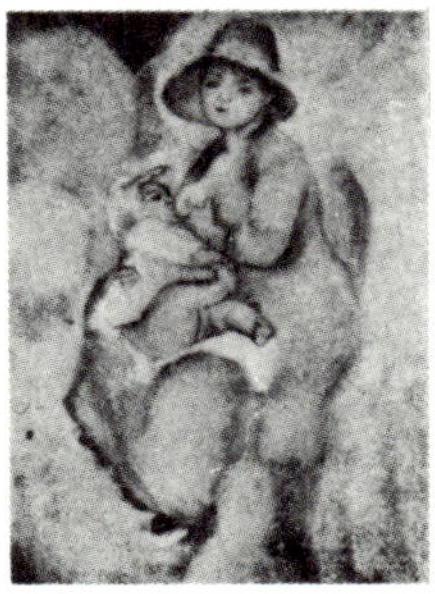

25. Motherhood – 1885. Private collection, London – *In this red chalk drawing with touches of white, Renoir's reaction to his period of crisis can again be seen: having understood that Impressionist techniques were no longer a suitable vehicle for the expression of his artistic ideas, the forms and techniques used in this drawing become almost forced.*

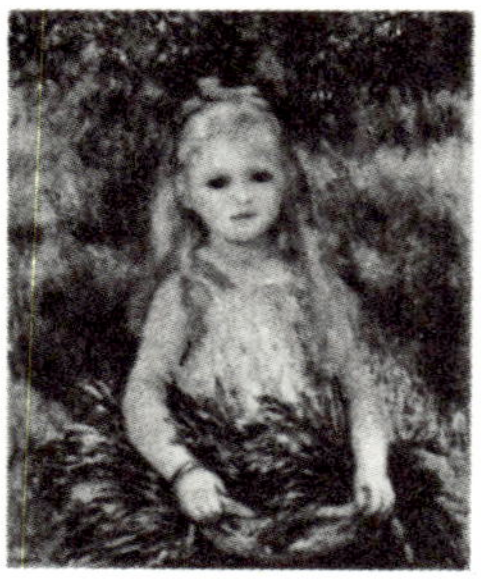

26. Little Girl with Sheaf of Grass and Wildflowers – 1888. Museu de Arte, São Paulo – *Even when he was seeking a way to supersede the limits of Impressionism, Renoir's love of everyday subjects allowed him to express himself very successfully in his scenes of country life. In this 1888 canvas the forms are set off by little touches of brighter colours.*

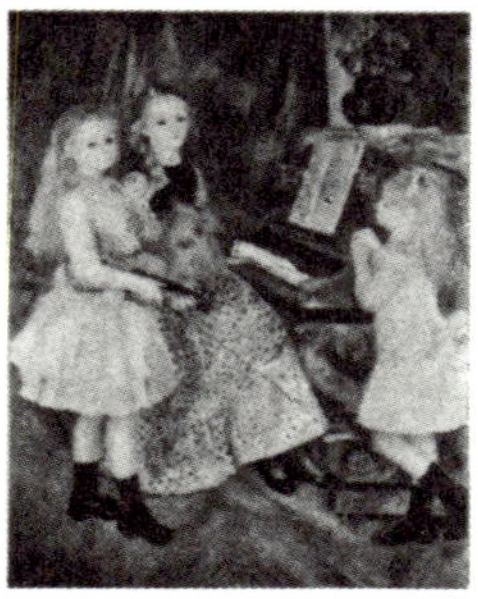

27. The Daughters of Catulle Mendès – 1888. The Hon. and Mrs. Walter H. Annenberg Collection, London – *This large composition, which was painted in 1888, is considered one of Renoir's masterpieces. He has overcome the crisis of the previous years and has developed a technique which enables him to see his subject through the eyes of Impressionism while at the same time never losing sight of the formal aspects that are essential to the composition.*

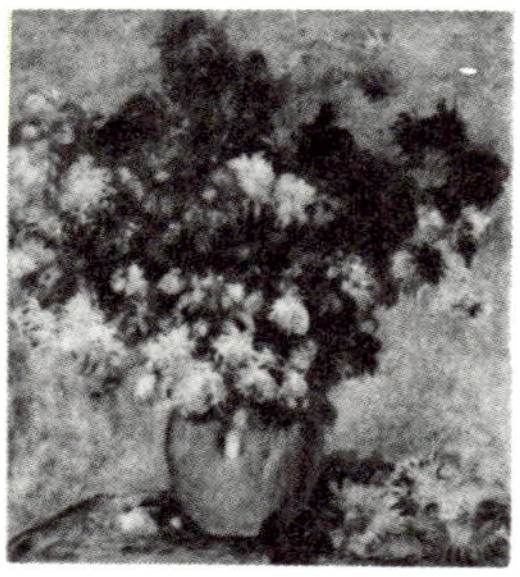

28. Vase of Chrysanthemums – Musée des Beaux-Arts, Rouen – *Like the previous picture, this painting dates back to the end of the nineteenth century and is a foretaste of the Cagnes period; a few flowers in a vase are sufficient to enable Renoir's eye and heart to create an unrivalled harmony of immense charm and freshness.*

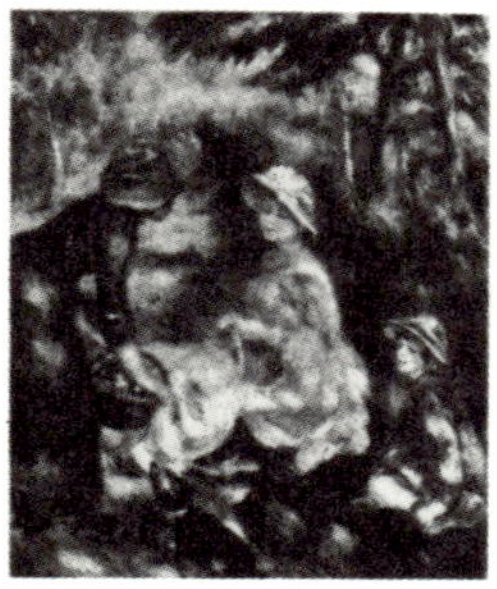

29. The Apple Vendor – 1890. Cleveland Museum of Art (Leonard C. Hanna Jr. Collection), Cleveland – *Renoir made several different versions of this picture, painted during the summer of 1890. In a delicate Impressionist atmosphere, the artist has painted his young wife with their eldest son, Pierre, and their nephew, Edmond, all seated on the grass.*

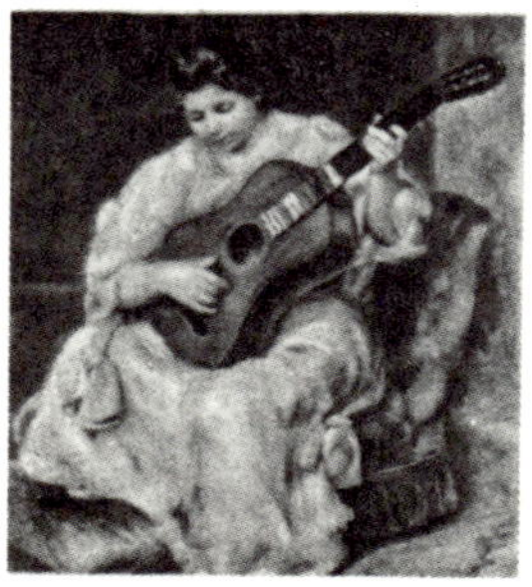

30. Woman Playing the Guitar – Musée des Beaux-Arts, Lyons – *This painting, which dates back to the end of the nineteenth century, shows the outcome of Renoir's plastic and structural research: his technique is more supple and fluid and has therefore acquired greater density than during the Impressionist period.*

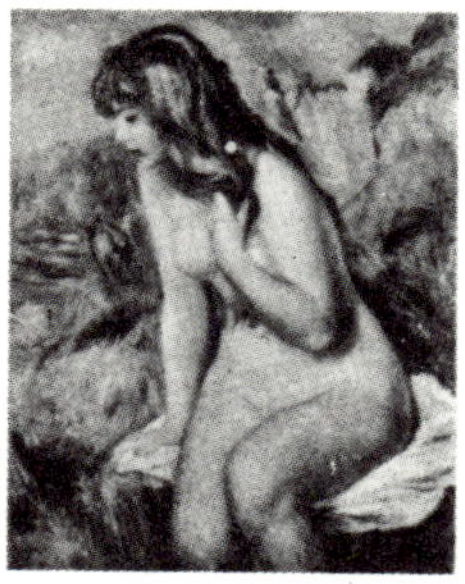

31. Bather Sitting on a Rock – 1892. Private collection, Paris – *This was one of Renoir's favourite themes and several versions of it exist. In this canvas, painted in 1892, the artist is still exploring the theme but it is already possible to see how the luminous atmosphere has been perfectly integrated with the figure and the slightly blurred outlines of the background.*

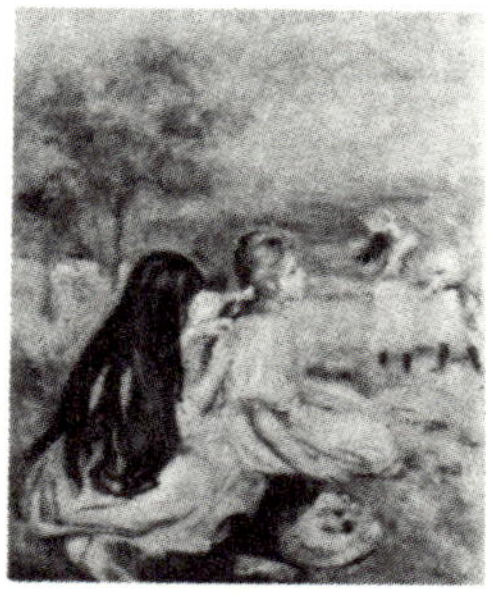

32. Girls by the Seaside – 1894. Baron Louis de Chollet Collection, Fribourg (Switzerland) – *Free from the harshness of the portraits painted during Renoir's period of crisis, this 1894 canvas is full of bright colours which blend harmoniously with all the elements of the composition and take nothing away from the definition of the forms. The broken brushstrokes add to the plasticity of the whole.*

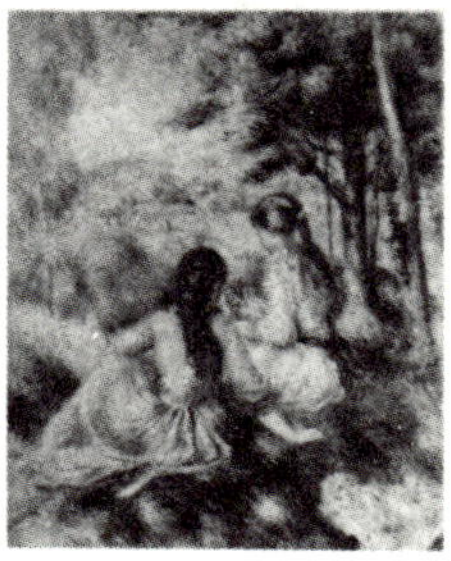

33. In the Meadow, or Gathering Flowers – 1890. Metropolitan Museum of Art, New York – *In this 1890 canvas Renoir develops an original style which enables him to combine Impressionist concepts with his own personal style. The light causes the figures to stand out against the surrounding landscape.*

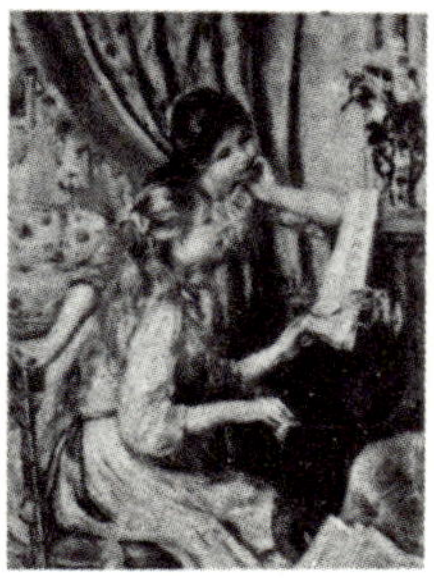

34. At the Piano – 1892. Musée d'Orsay, Paris – *This is probably the last of several variations on the same theme all painted during the same year. The minute description of the interior, the dresses and the faces of the girls in no way distract the observer since the light which fills the whole composition emphasizes the gentle charm of the scene.*

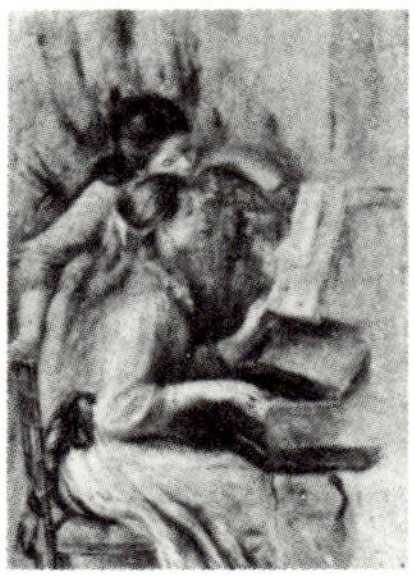

35. At the Piano – 1892. Madame Jean Walter Collection, Paris – *During the last years of the nineteenth century Renoir often painted whole series of paintings representing one or two figures. These variations on the same theme were the expression of the research being carried out by the artist during this period into the painting of portraits and nudes. Despite the lack of detail, this 1892 canvas is an example of Renoir's Impressionist technique.*

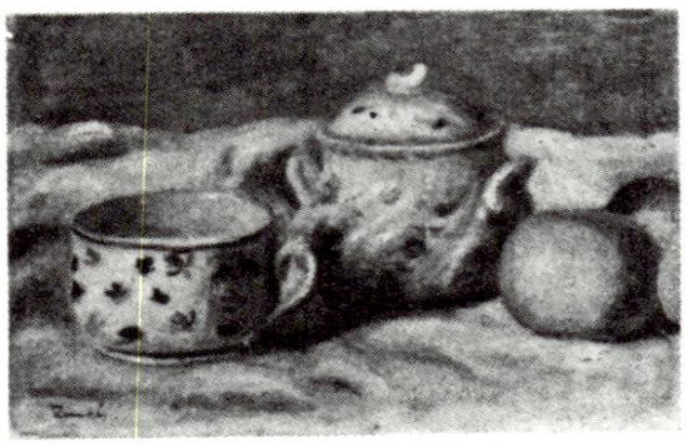

36. Still-Life with Cup and Sugar Bowl – 1904. Private collection, Paris – *Few artists loved the simple things of everyday life as much as Renoir. His many paintings of everyday objects bear witness to this and express the artist's inner warmth.*

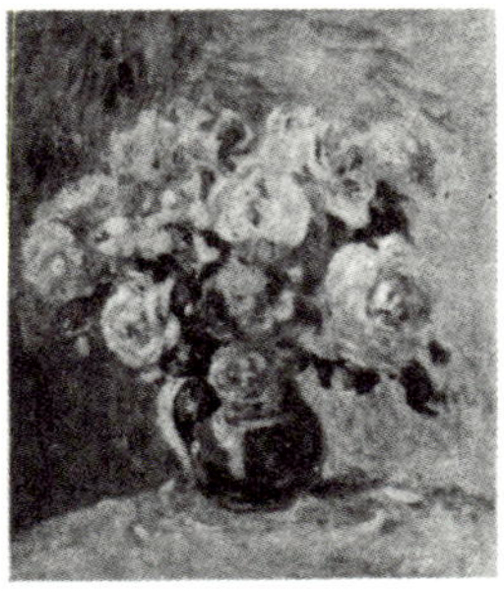

37. Flowers in a Vase – 1901. Private collection, Ireland – *During the last years of his life Renoir painted numerous floral compositions. They were experiments with colours and colour shades. Roses interested him particularly due to their affinity with the flesh tones he used to paint the human body.*

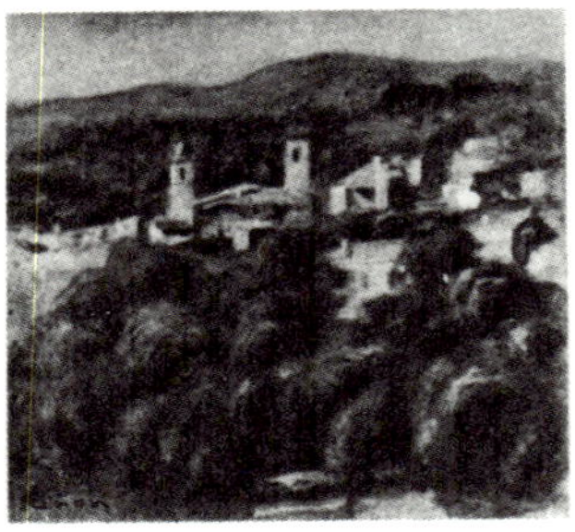

38. Cros-de-Cagnes – 1905. Private collection, Lausanne – *During the last period of his artistic production, Renoir painted landscapes with deeper colours like red or superimposed greens and blues which are in perfect harmony with the rest of the work.*

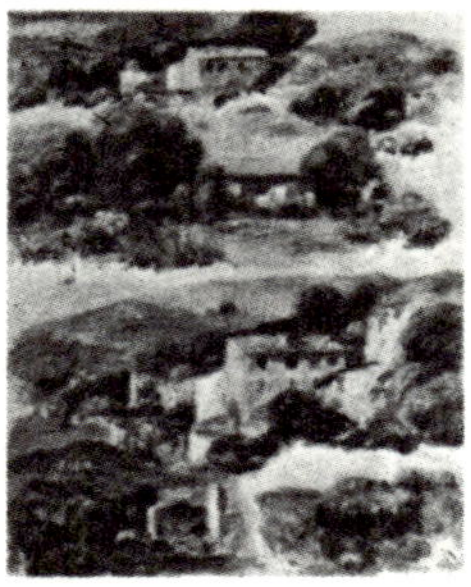

39. Houses at Cagnes – 1905. Private collection, Paris – *During his stay in Cagnes, where he spent the last years of his life, Renoir often painted the surrounding landscape with its houses and greenery. In this 1905 study the deep hues typical of the south of France are reproduced by means of bright, warm colours.*

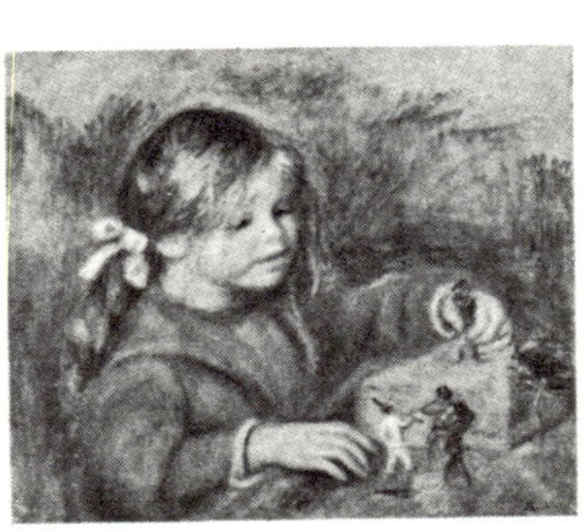

40. Claude Renoir Playing with His Toys – c. 1906. Madame Jean Walter Collection, Paris – *Family life was always a source of inspiration for Renoir. One of his favourite models was his youngest son Claude, nicknamed Coco, whom the artist painted in all kinds of spontaneous poses, intent on discovering the joys of life.*

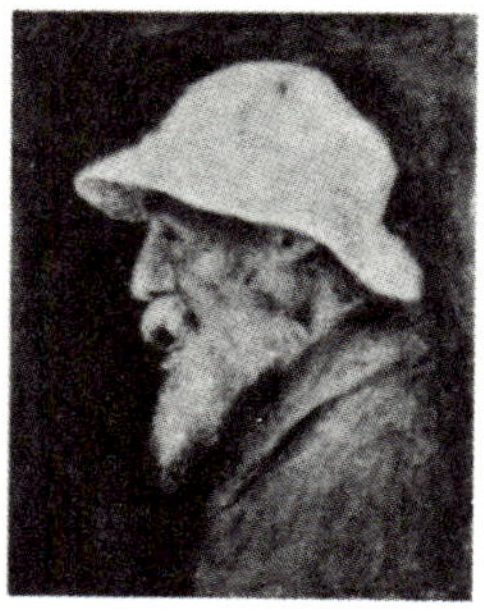

41. Self-Portrait with a White Hat – 1910. Durand-Ruel Collection, Paris – *The gentle serenity expressed in this 1910 self-portrait perfectly reflects Renoir's open, happy attitude to life. It was his own special vision of the world that enabled him to transmit the joyous harmony of nature in all his paintings.*

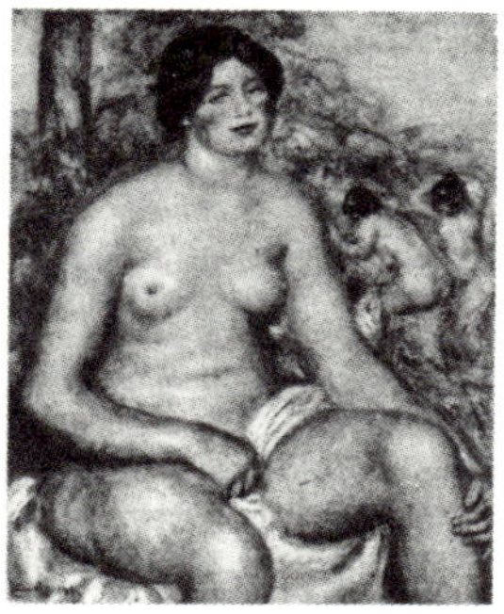

42. Seated Bather – 1914. Art Institute, Chicago – *This is one of the most important paintings of his last period. Characterized by the large scale of the composition, the painting is almost entirely taken up by the seated bather and contains an infinite variety of nuances of colour, all arising from the same basic flesh tones.*

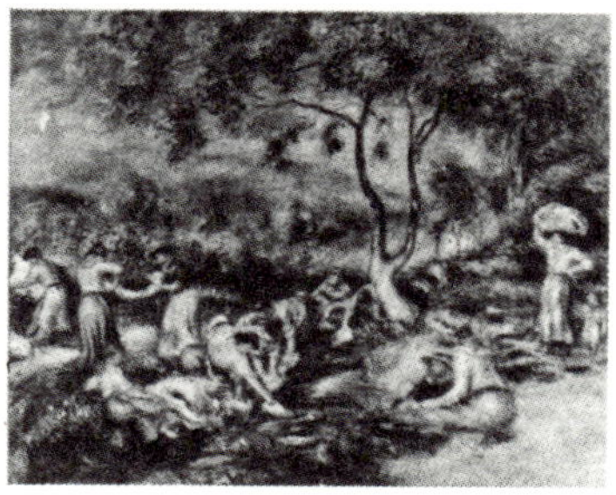

43. Washerwomen at Cagnes – 1912. Private collection, Paris – *The last period of Renoir's life was the richest, the most immediate, and the most mature from an artistic point of view. In addition to female nudes (the real protagonists of his art), he painted canvases like this one (dated 1912), where an everyday scene is depicted with a sureness of touch and an intensity of colour that has never since been surpassed.*

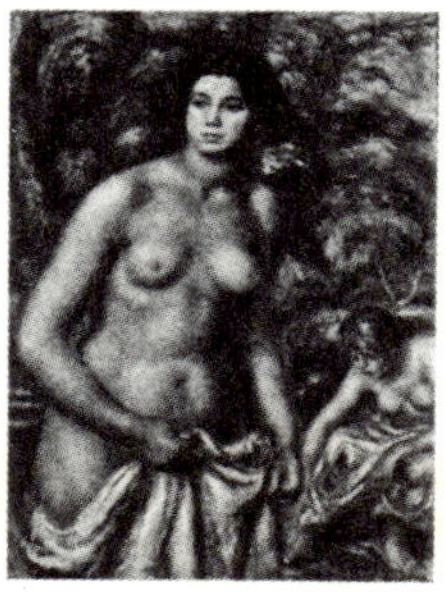

44. Madeleine Bruno, or The Two Bathers – 1916. Private collection, Paris – *At the height of his artistic maturity, in this 1916 painting, Renoir has recaptured with effortless ease the full-bodied forms and graceful gestures of ancient Classical statuary. The perfect fusion of the figure with the background creates the pantheist synthesis to which Renoir had always aspired.*

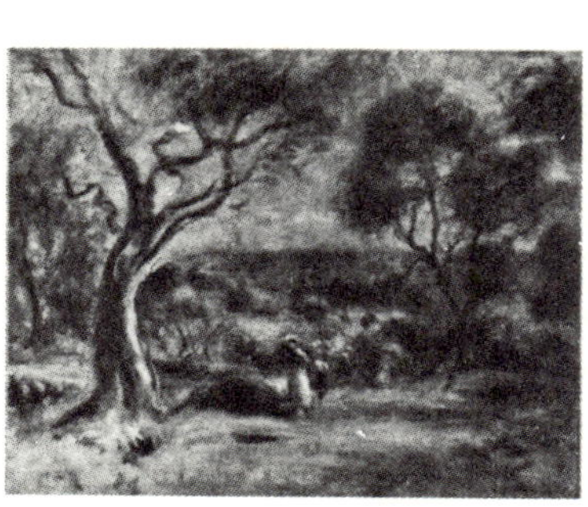

45. Promenade along the Sea – Museum of Modern Art (Grassi Collection), Milan – *Renoir's passionate response to landscapes which inspired him is summarized in the poetic interpretation given in this painting where the figures blend perfectly with the landscape to give a classical sense of serenity to the whole work.*

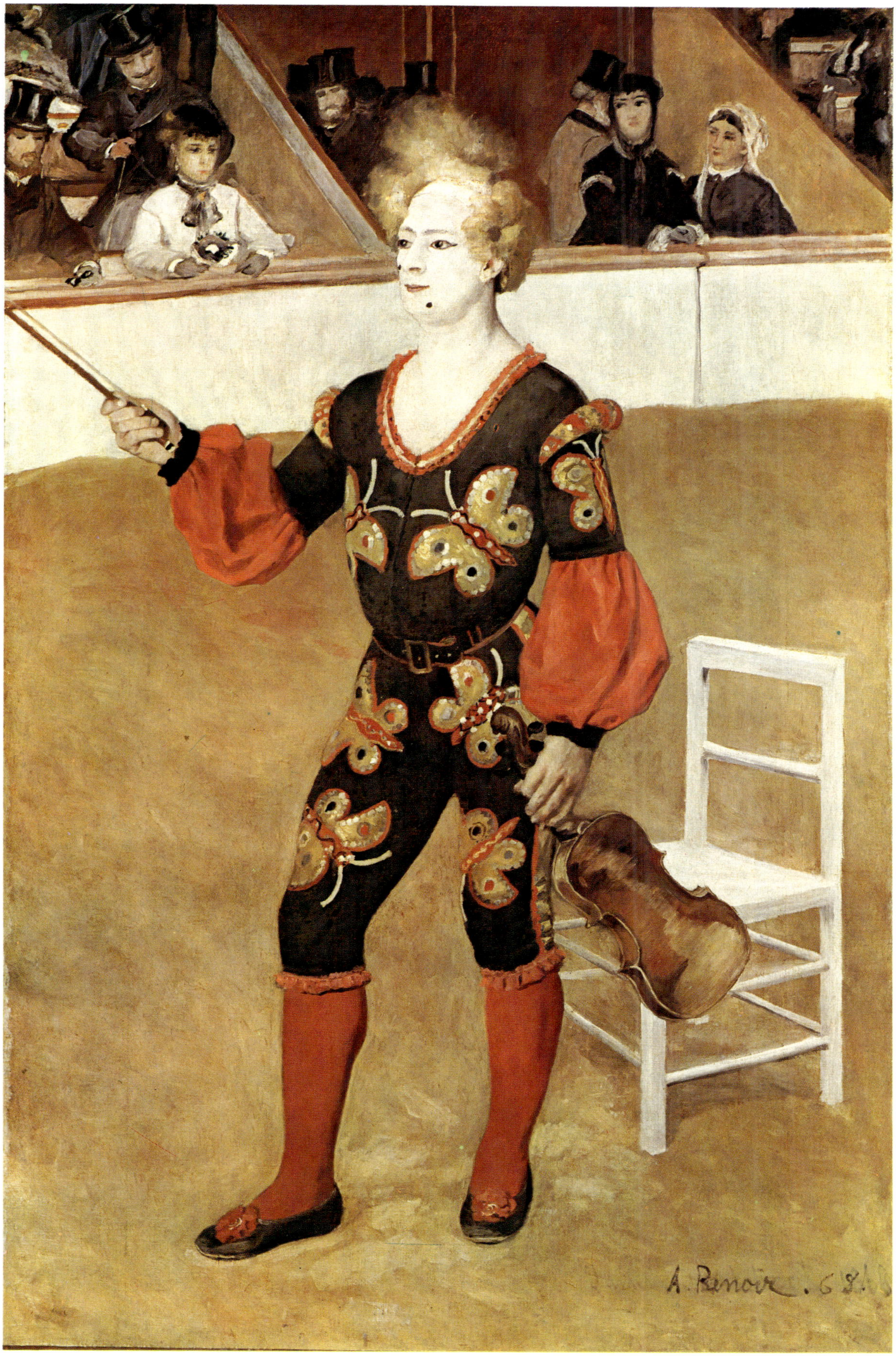

1. *The Clown – 1868. Rijksmuseum Kröller-Müller, Otterlo*

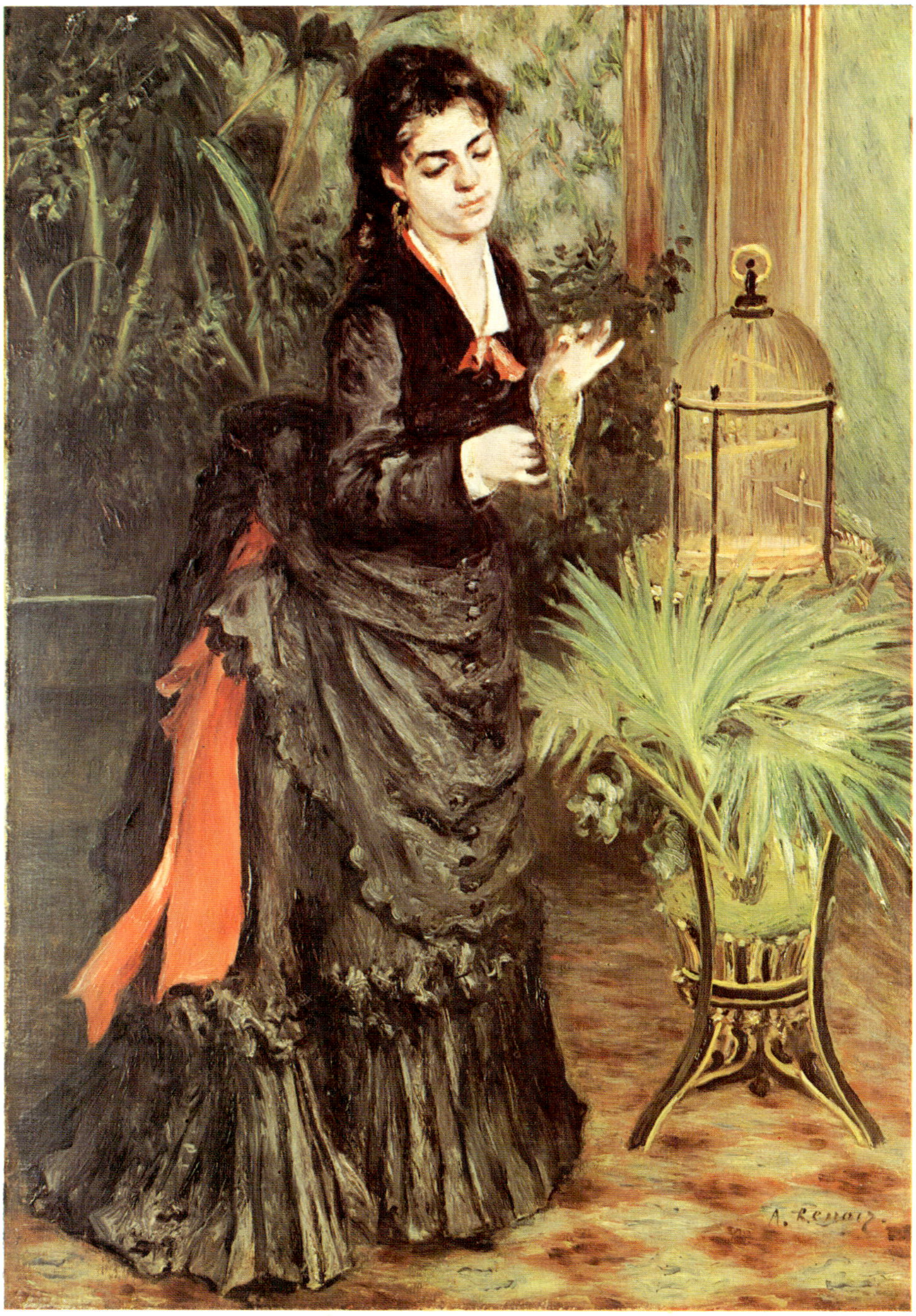

2. *Lady with a Parakeet* – 1871. Solomon R. Guggenheim Foundation (Tannhauser Collection), New York

3. *La Grenouillère* – 1869. National Museum, Stockholm

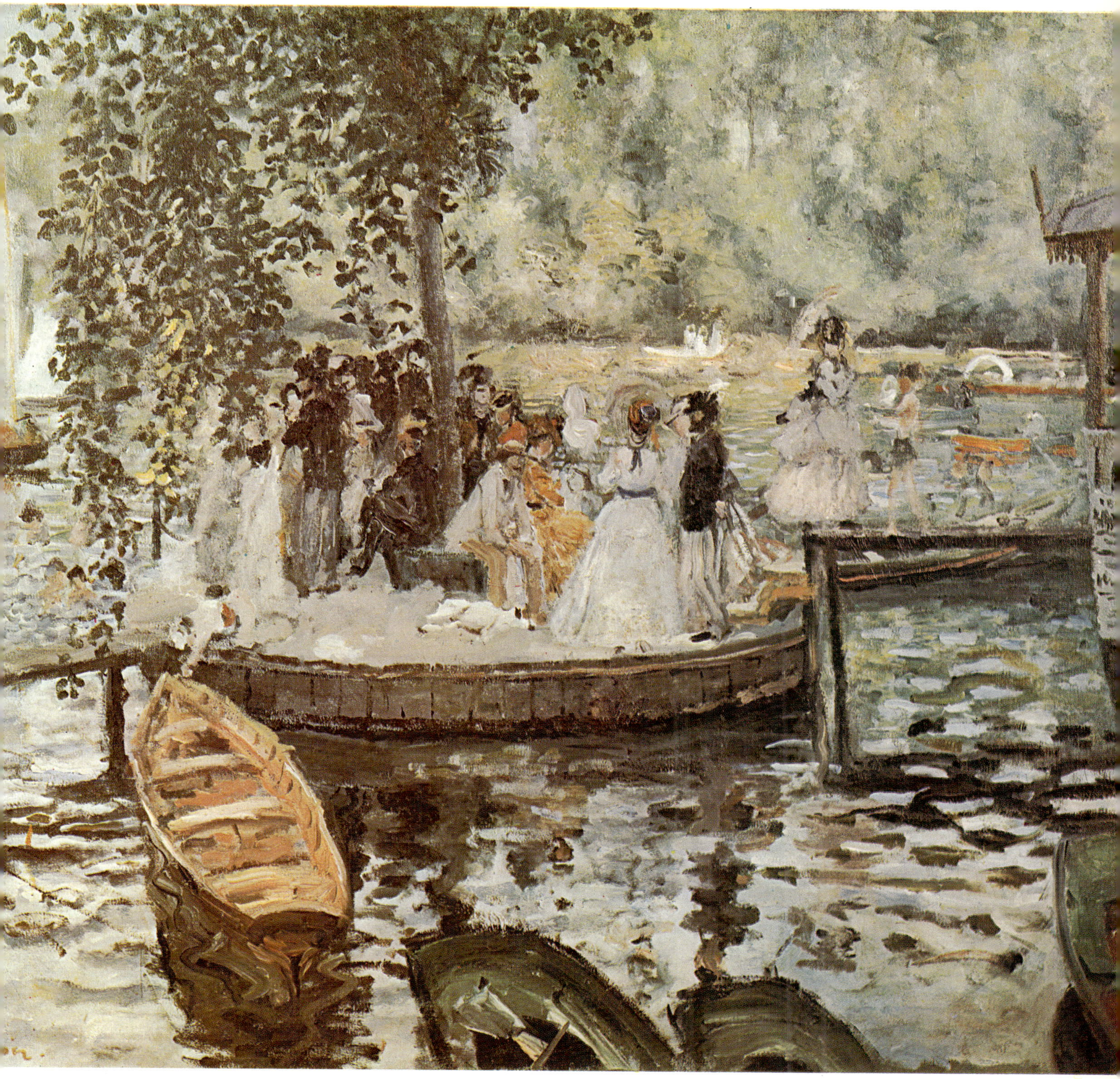

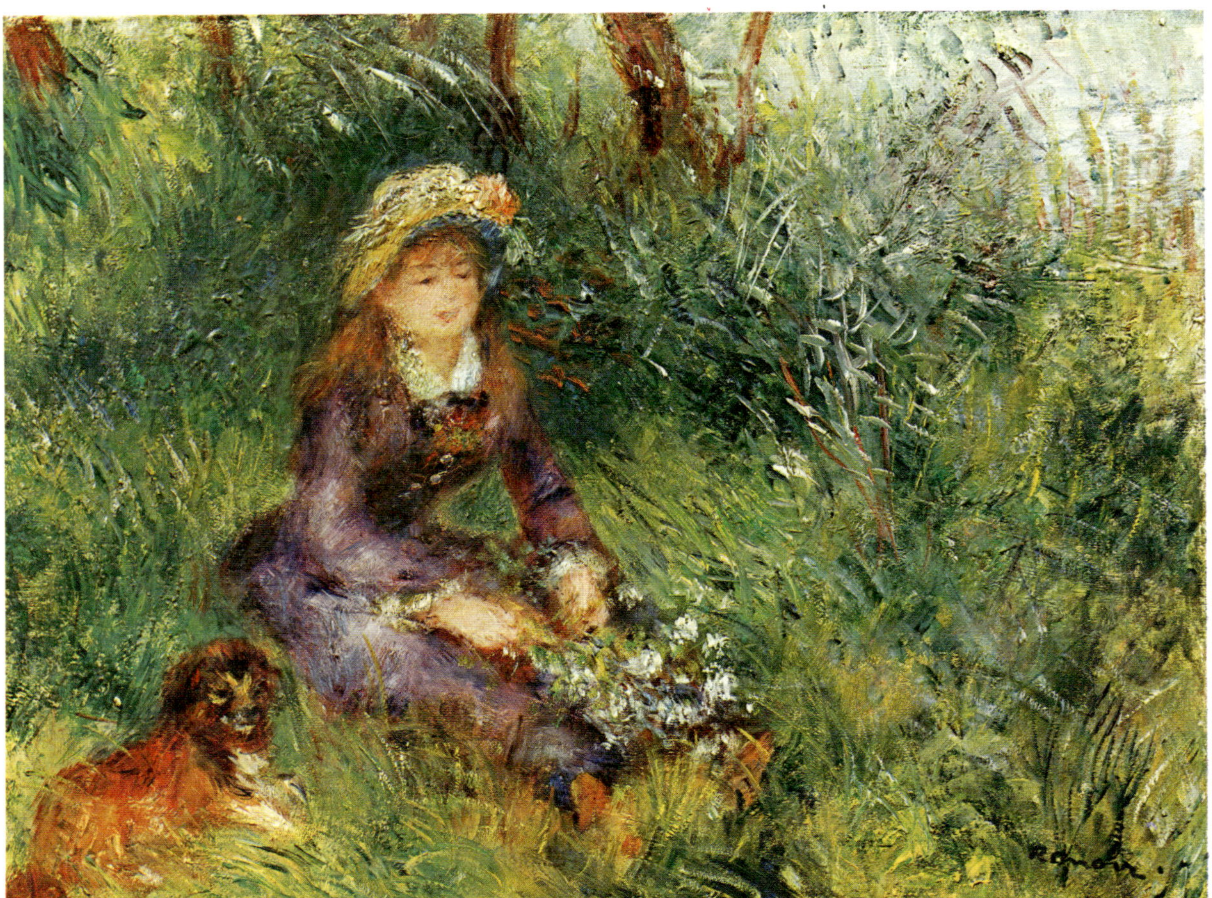

4. *Madame Renoir with her Dog* – 1880. Private collection, Paris

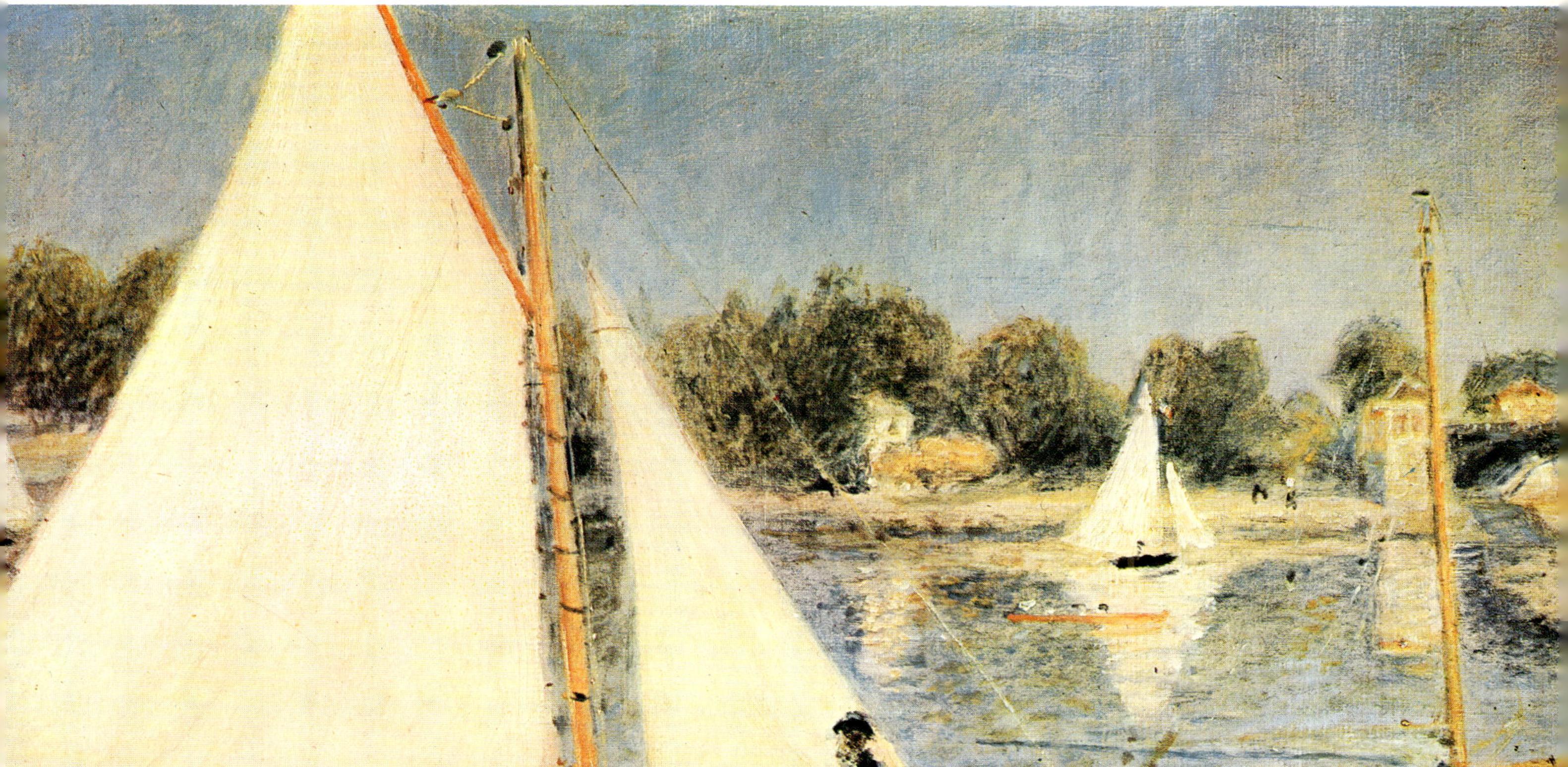

5. *The Seine at Argenteuil* – 1873-74. Portland Museum of Art, Oregon

6. *The Loge* – 1874. Courtauld Institute Galleries, London

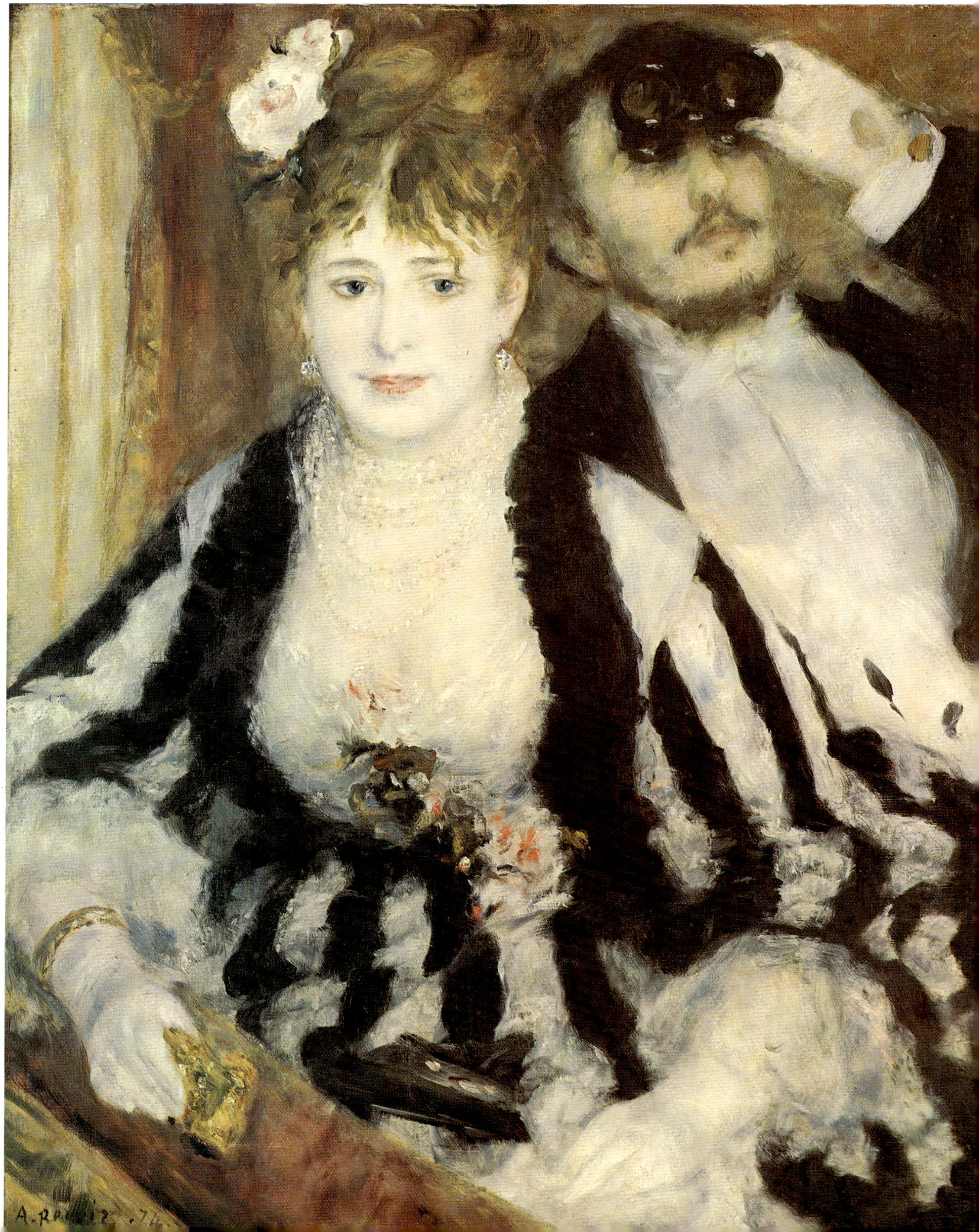

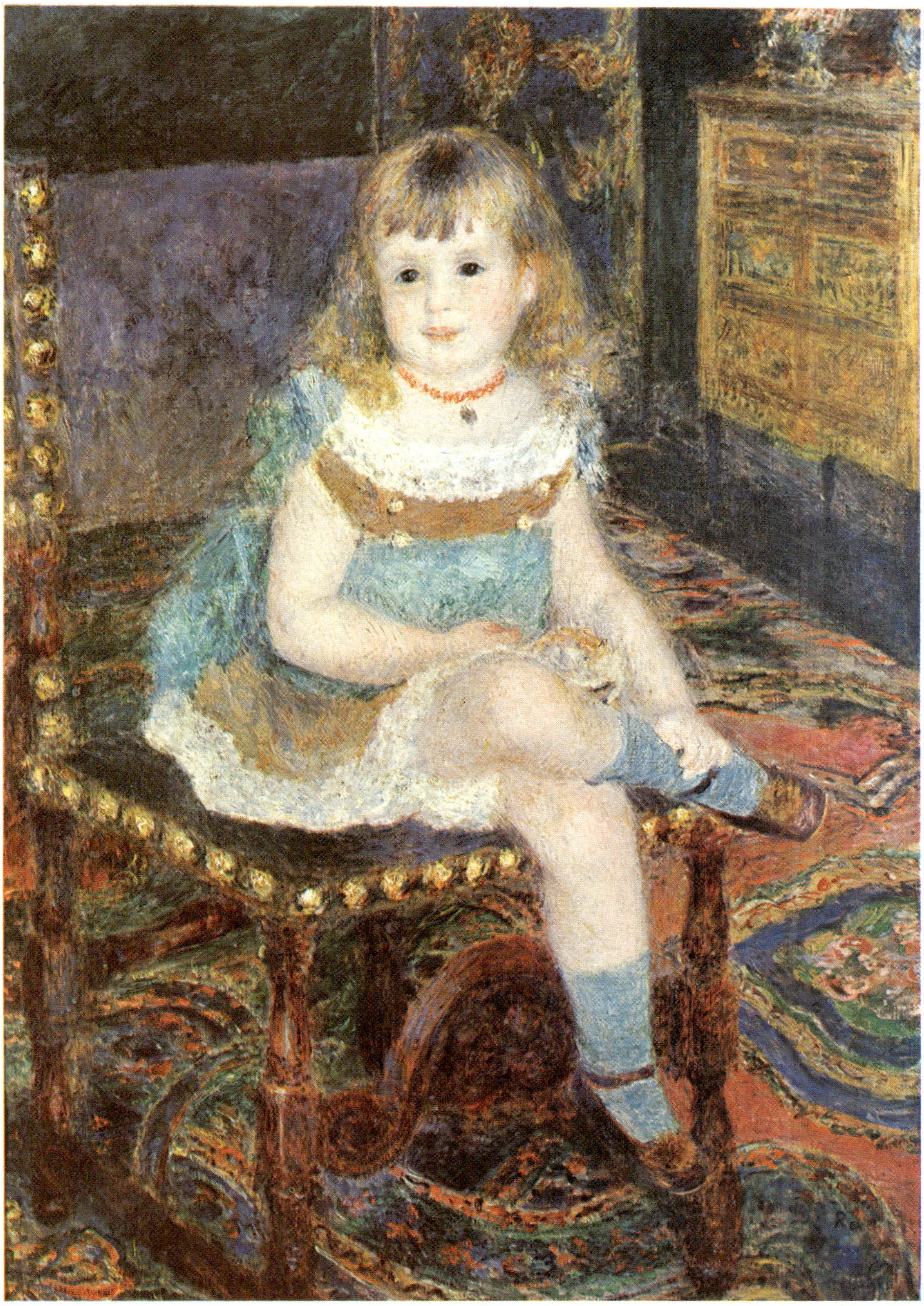

7. *Mademoiselle Georgette Charpentier Seated* – 1876. Private collection, New York

8. *Le Moulin de la Galette* – 1876. Musée d'Orsay, Paris

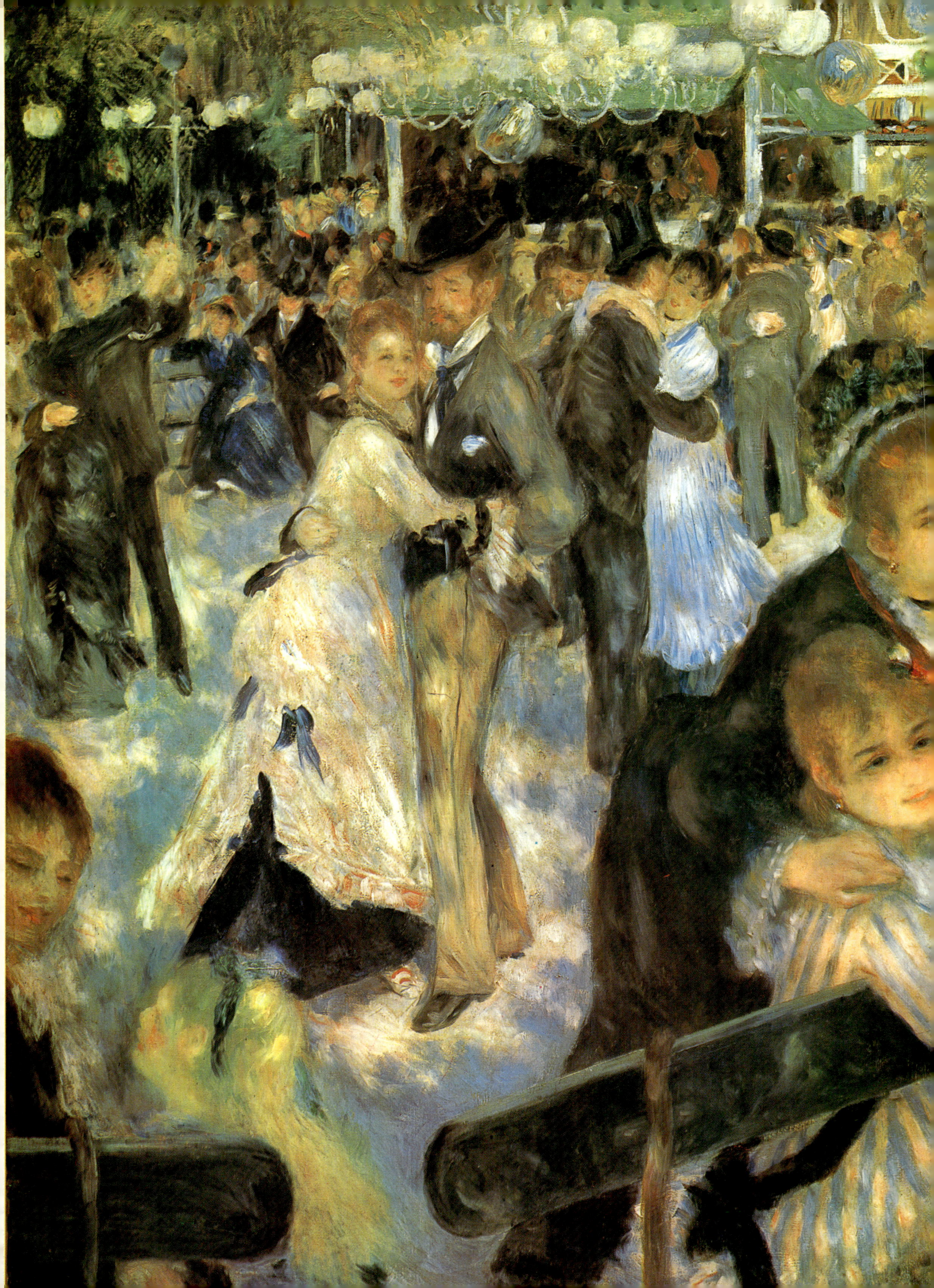

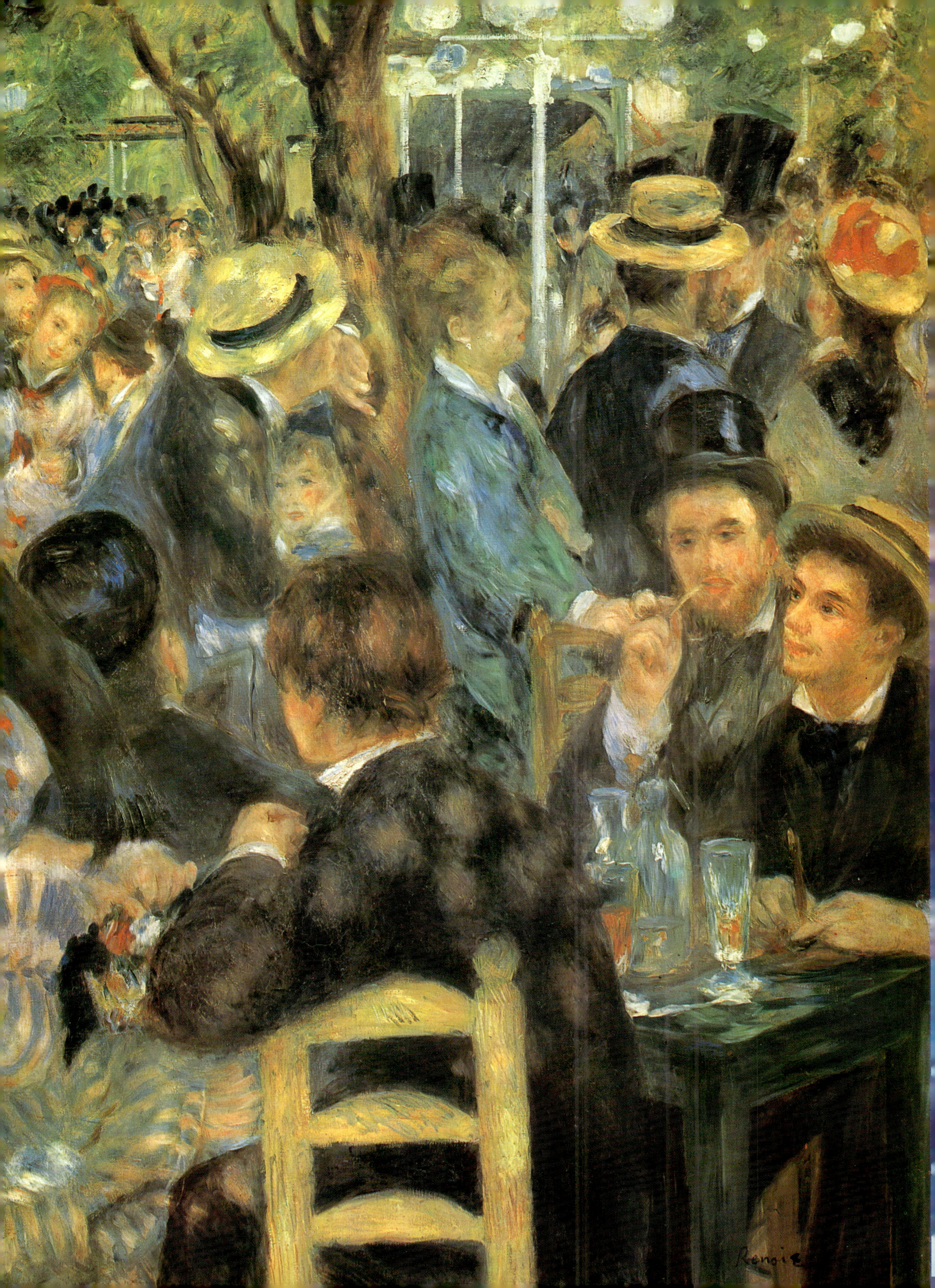

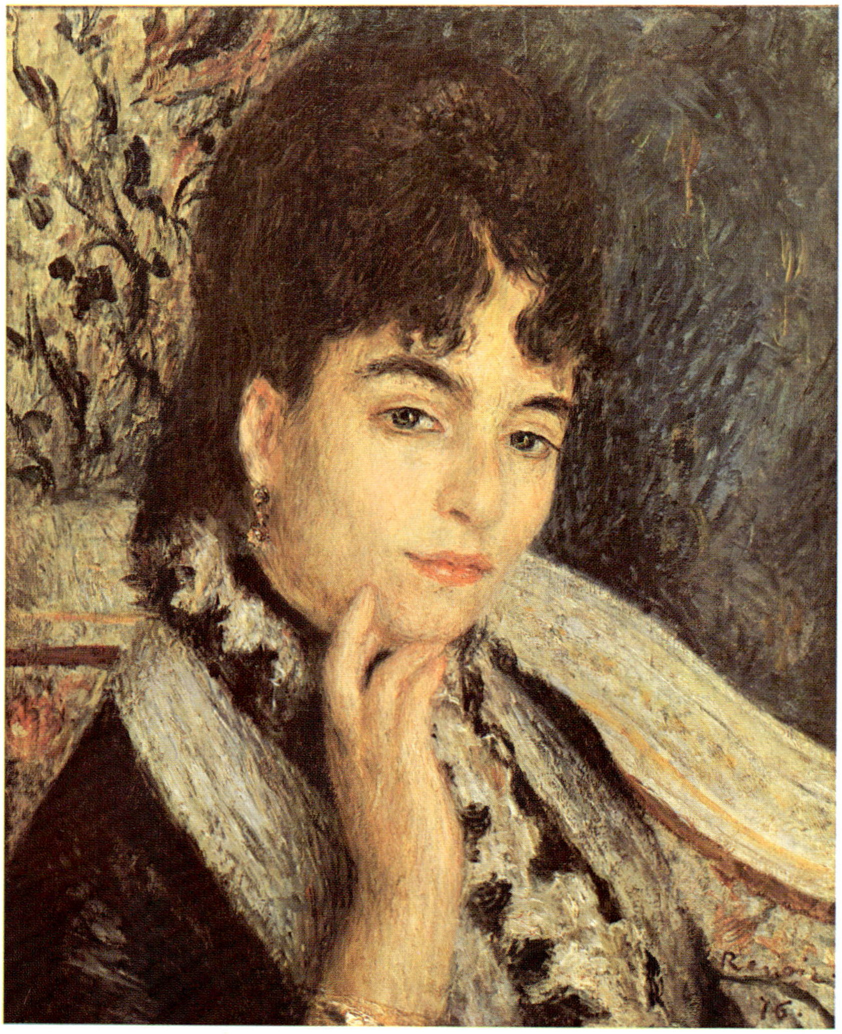

9. *Portrait of Madame Alphonse Daudet* – 1876. Musée du Louvre, Paris

10. *The Swing* – 1876. Musée du Louvre, Paris

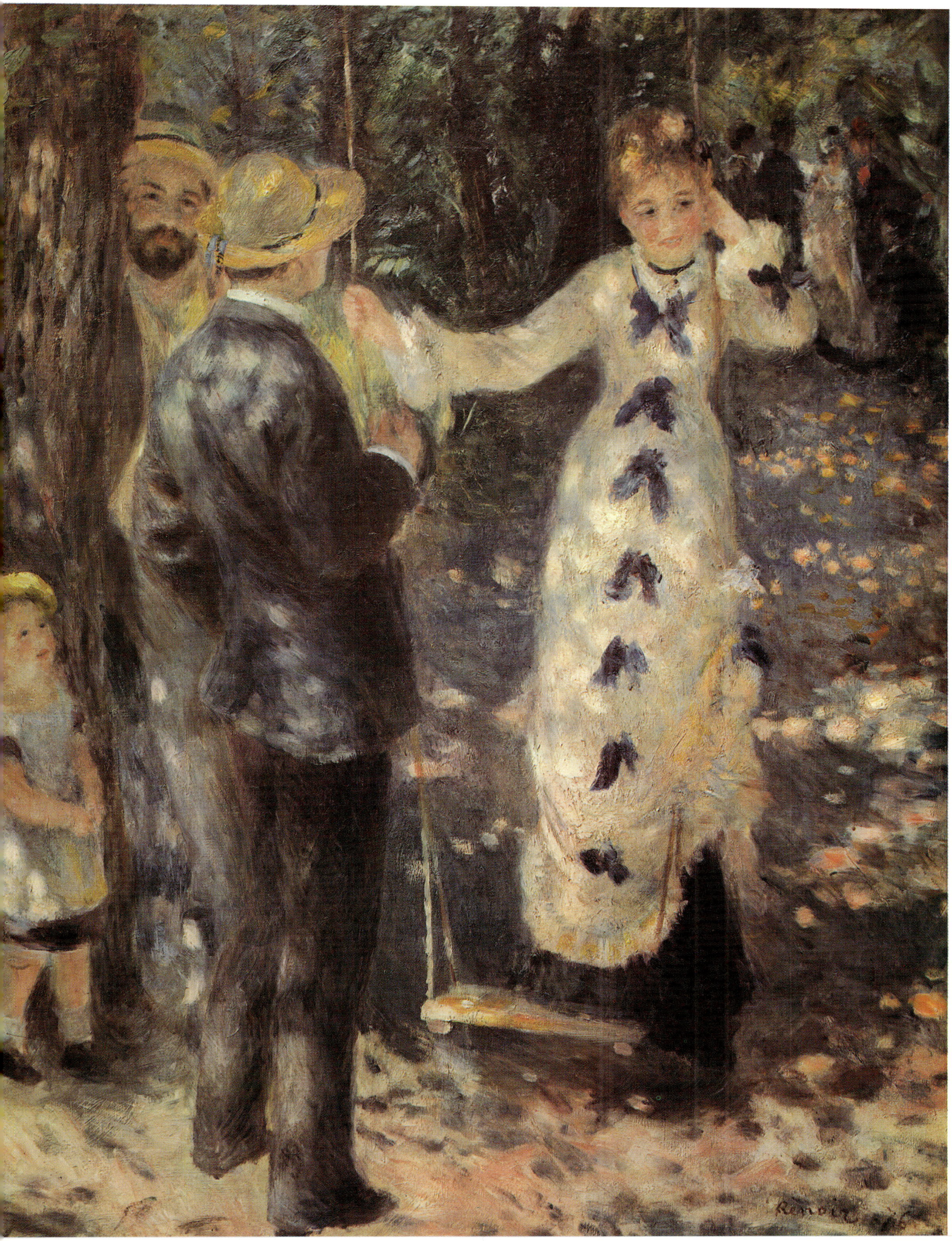

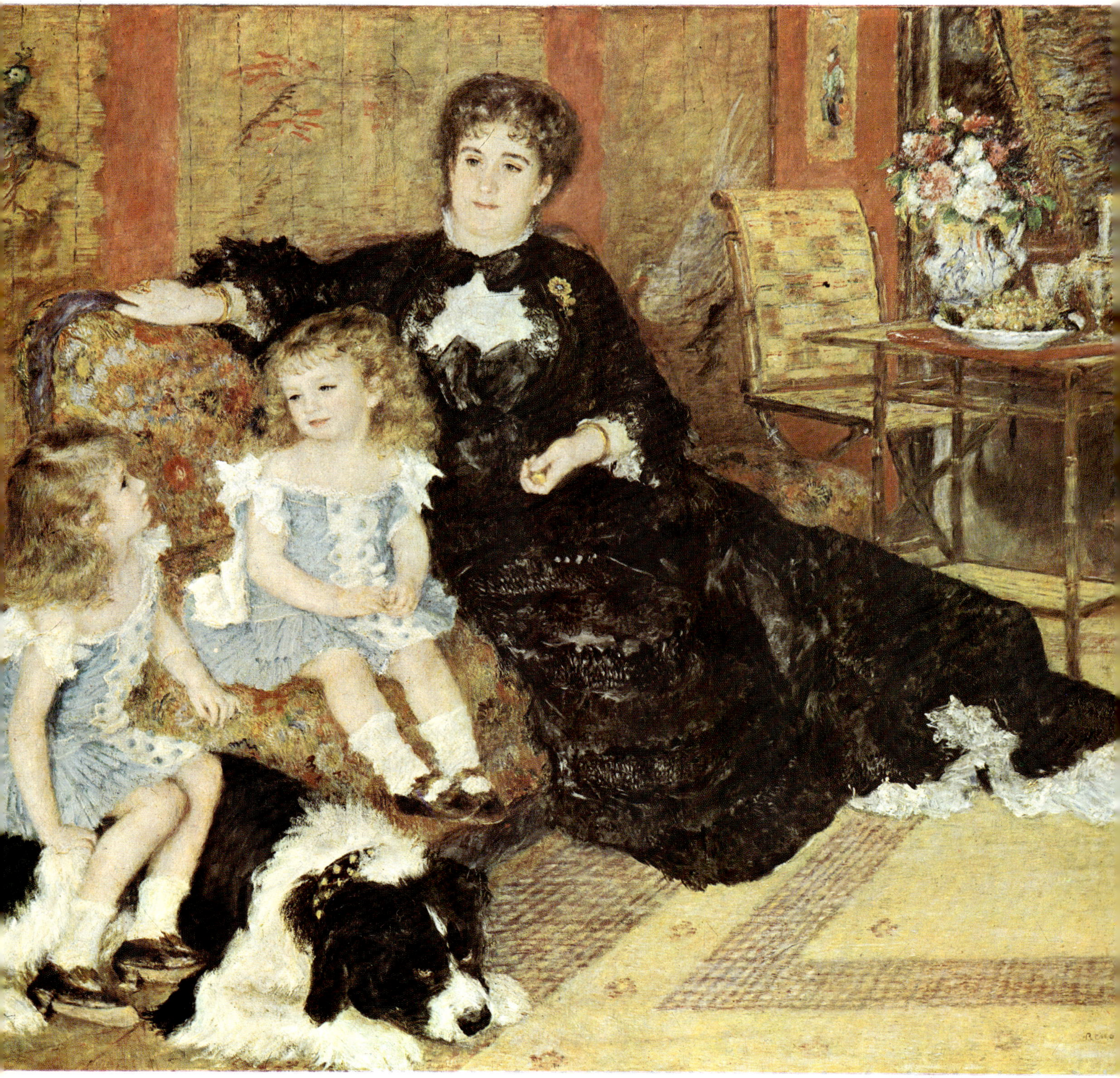

13. *Madame Georges Charpentier and Her Daughters* – 1878. Metropolitan Museum of Art (Wolfe Fund), New York

4. *Portrait of Madame Henriot* – c. 1877. National Gallery of Art (gift of Adèle R. Levy Fund Inc.), Washington, D.C.

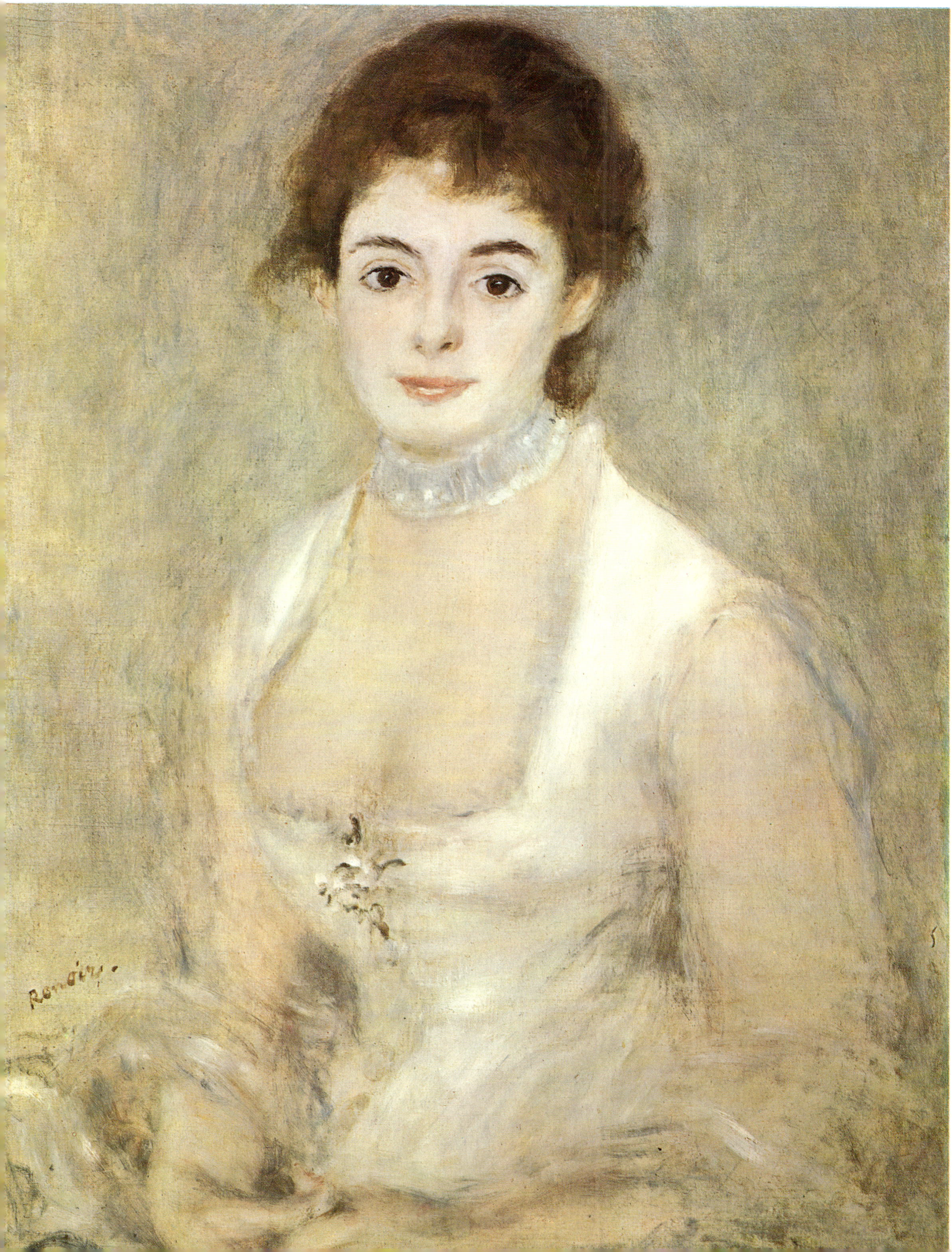

15. *The Luncheon of the Boating Party* – 1880-1881. Phillips Collection, Washington, D.C.

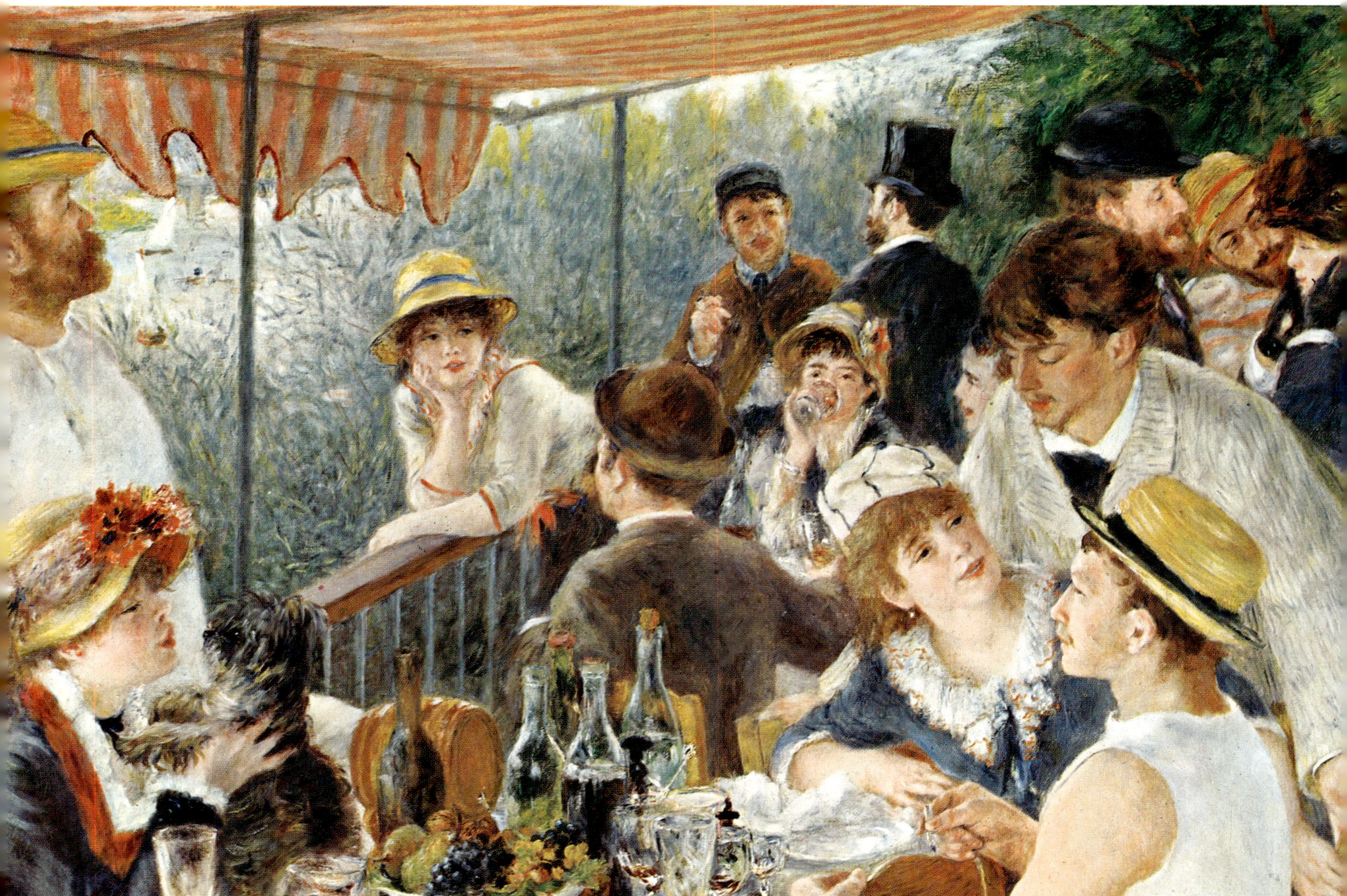

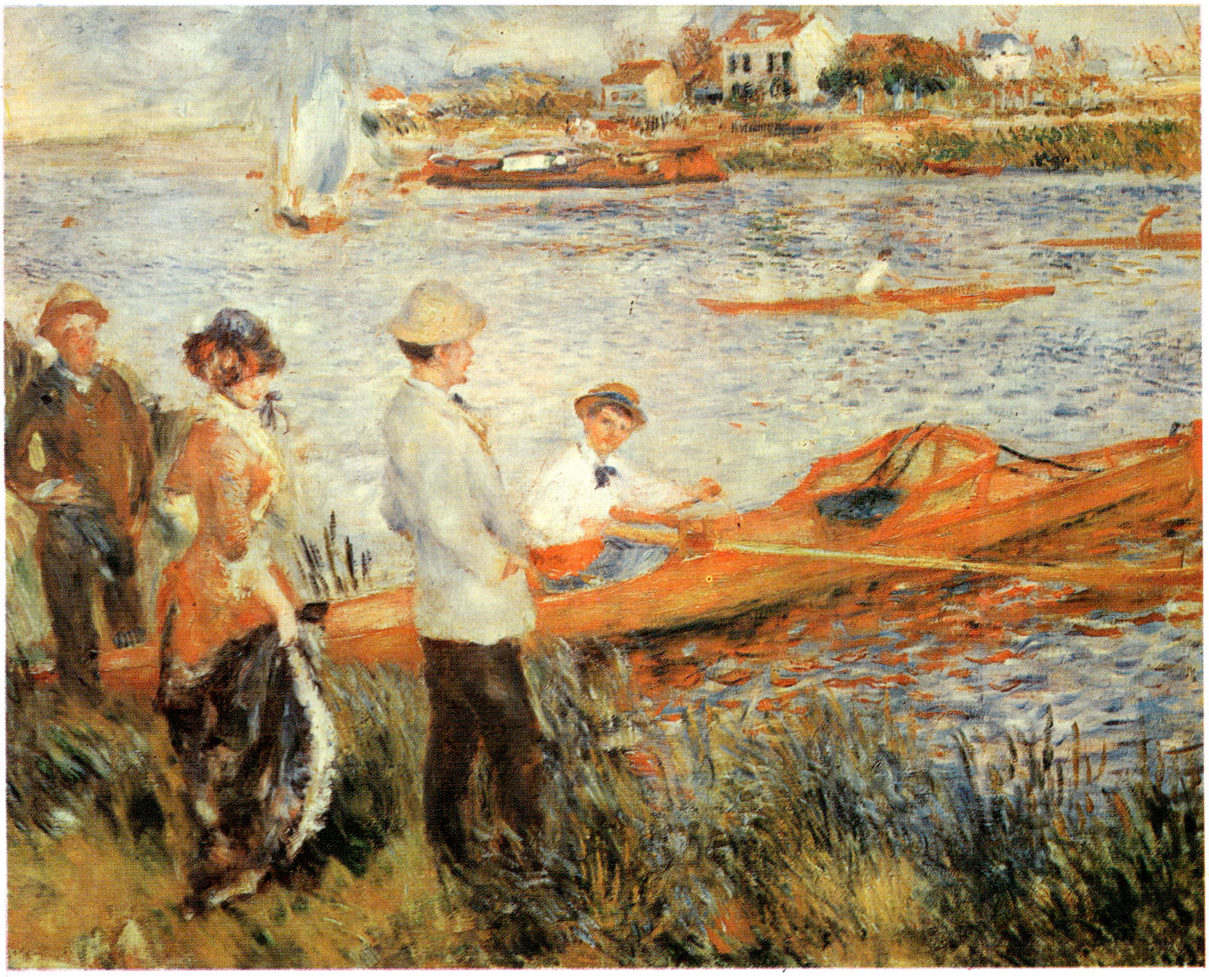

16. *Boating Party at Chatou* – 1879. National Gallery of Art, Washington, D.C.

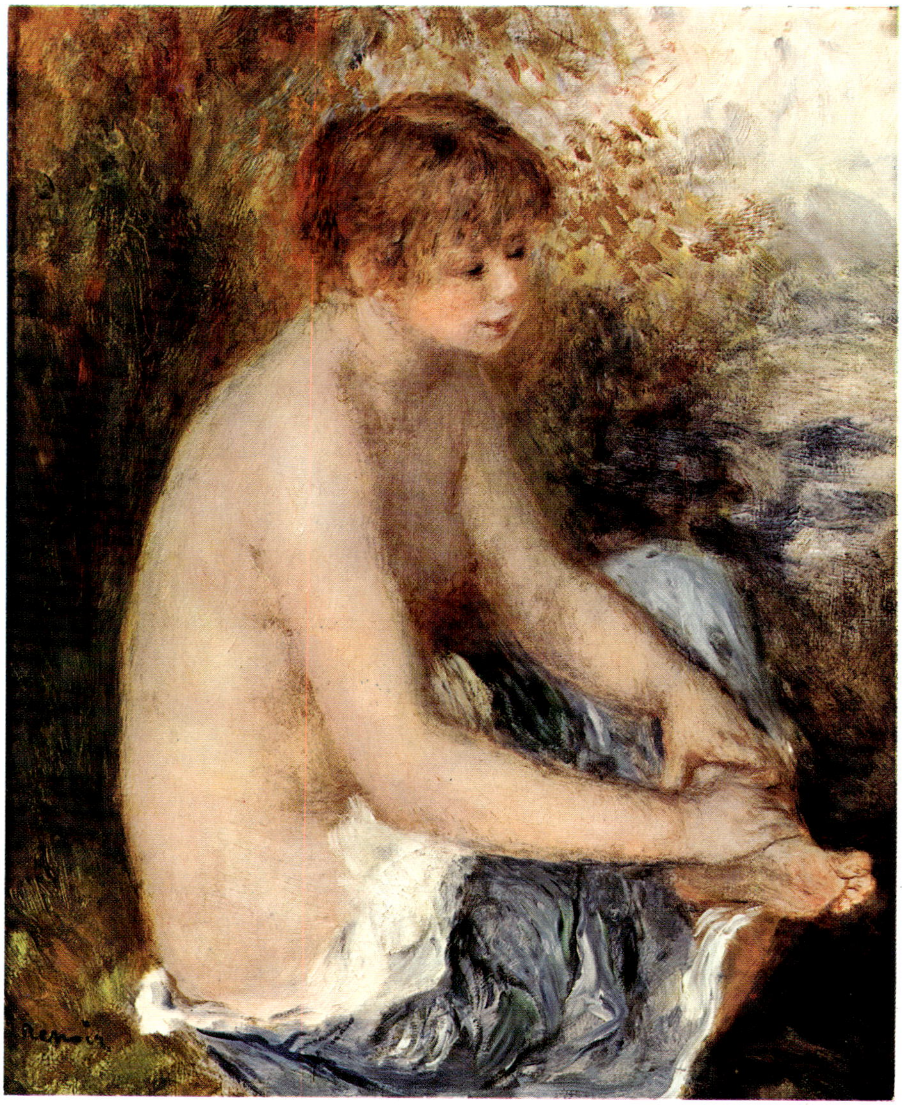

17. *Little Blue Nude* – 1879. The Albright-Knox Art Gallery, Buffalo (N.Y.)

18. *The Blond Bather* – 1881-1882. Private collection, Turin

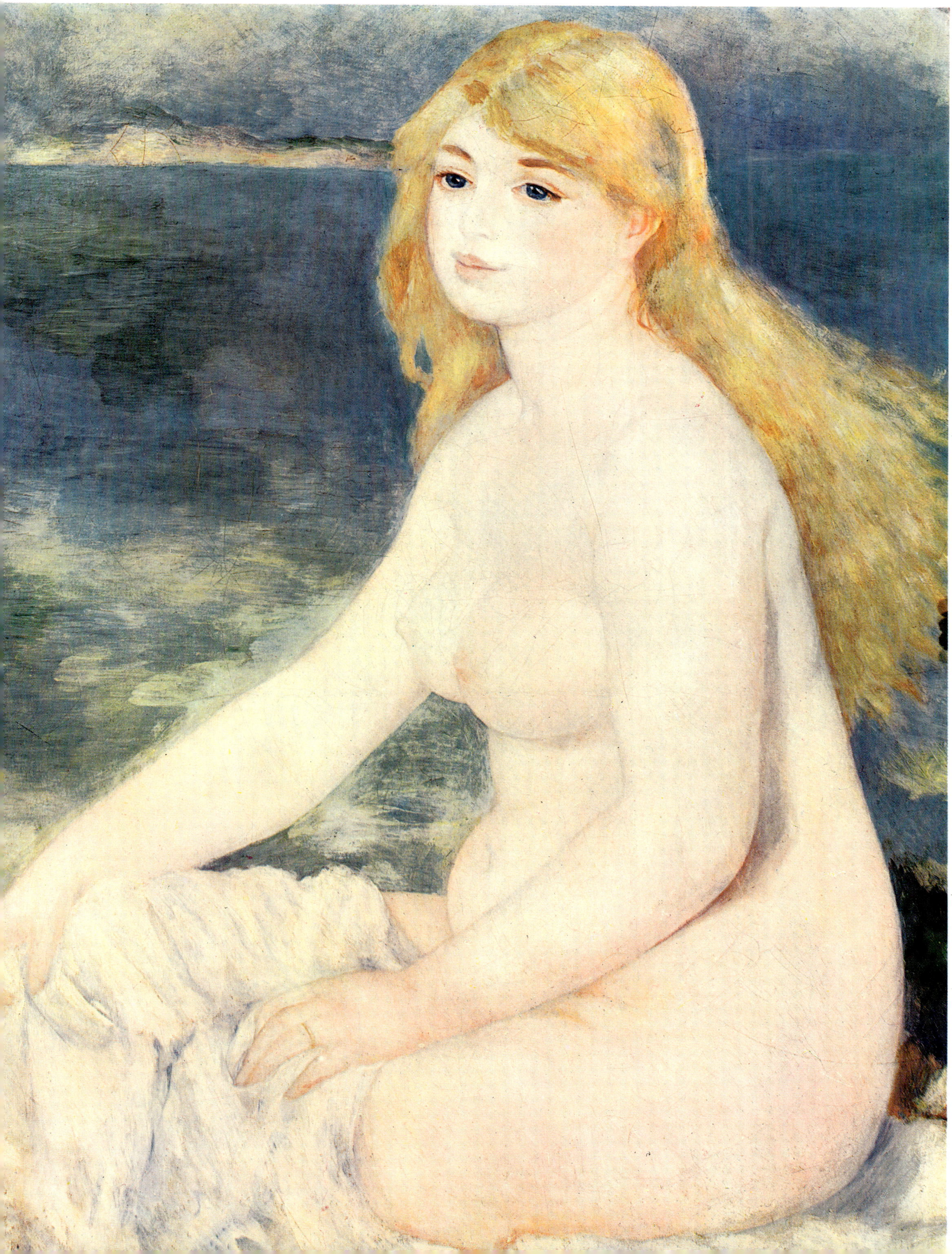

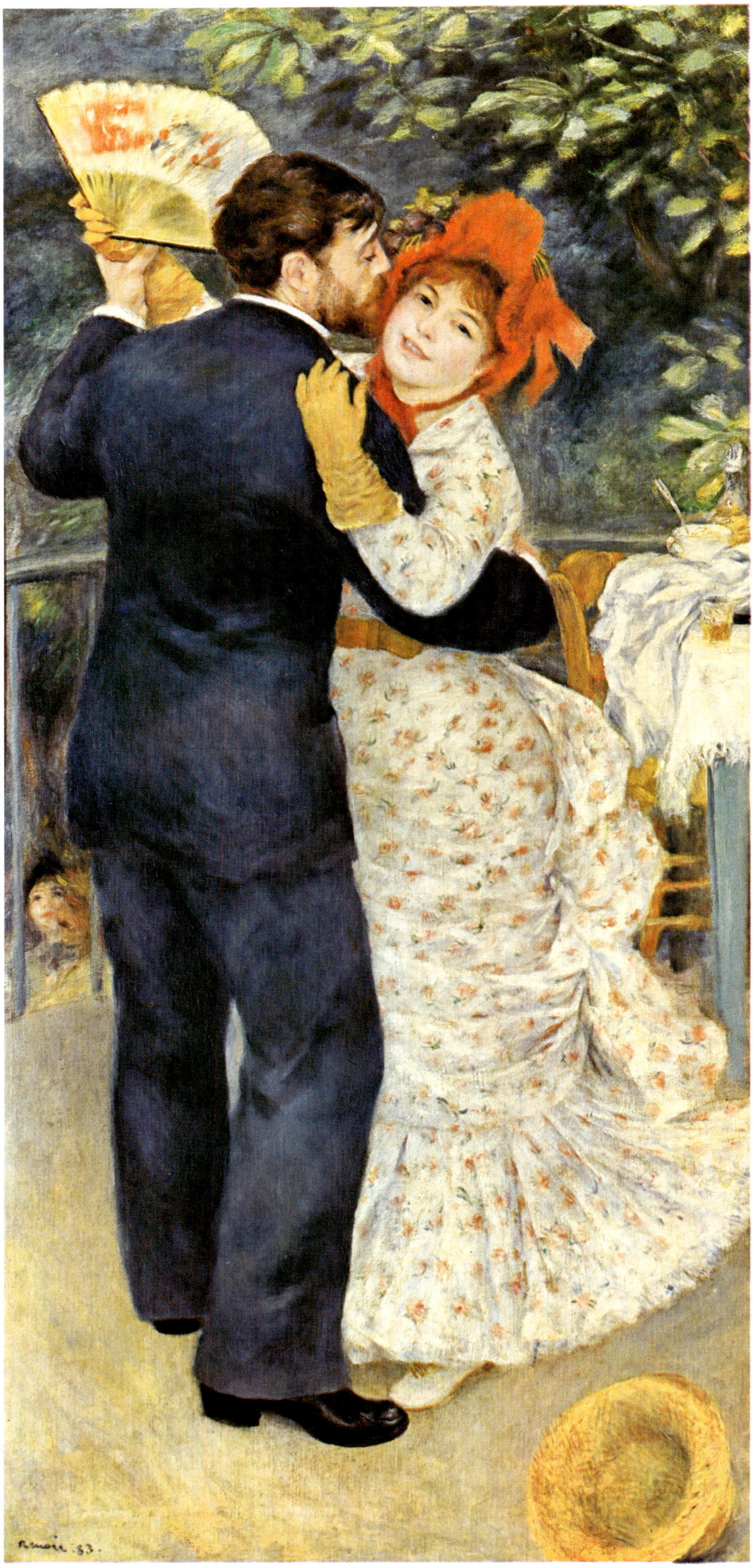

19. *Dancing in the Country* – 1883. Musée d'Orsay, Paris

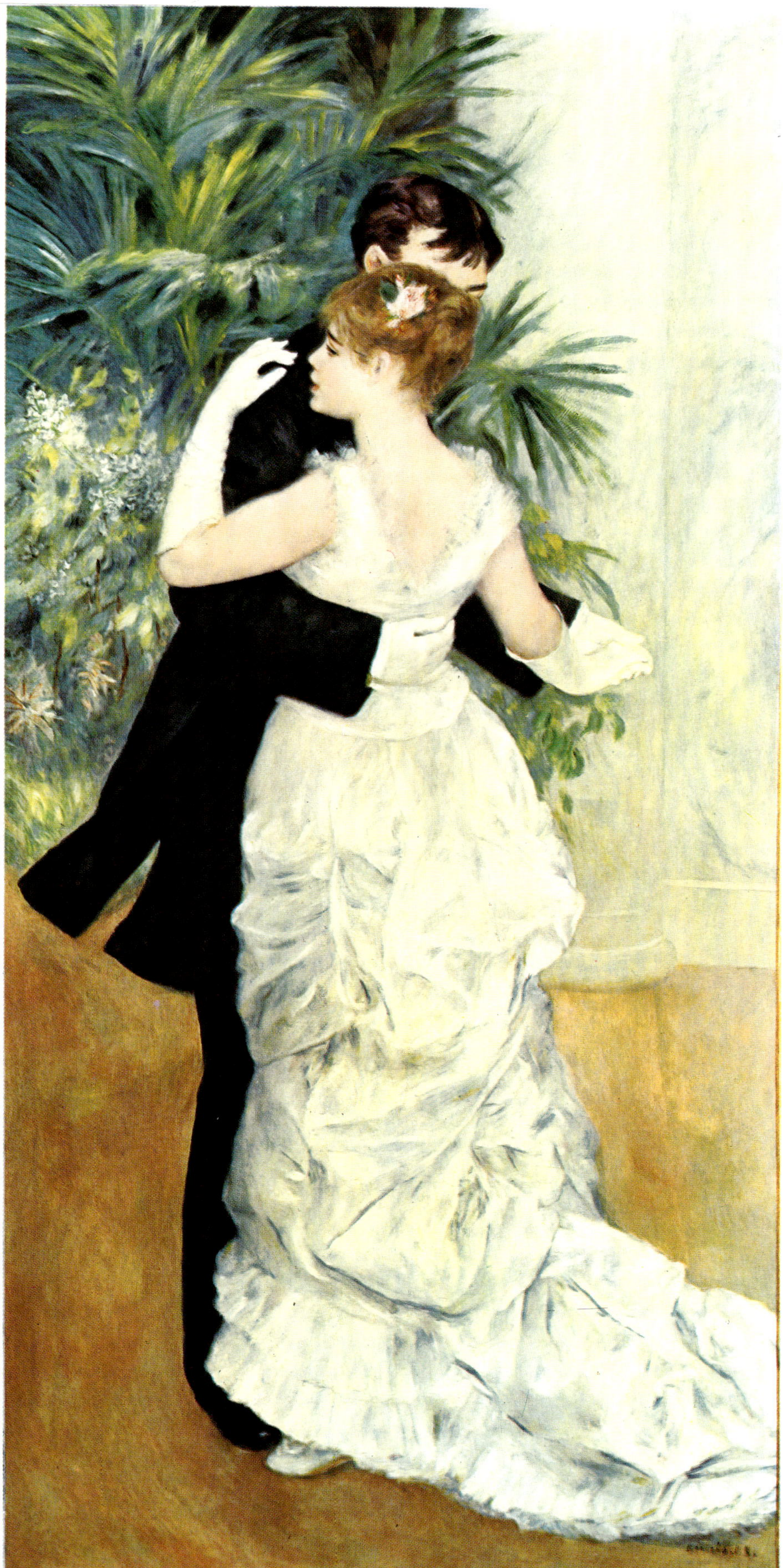

20. *Dancing in Town* – 1883. Musée d'Orsay, Paris

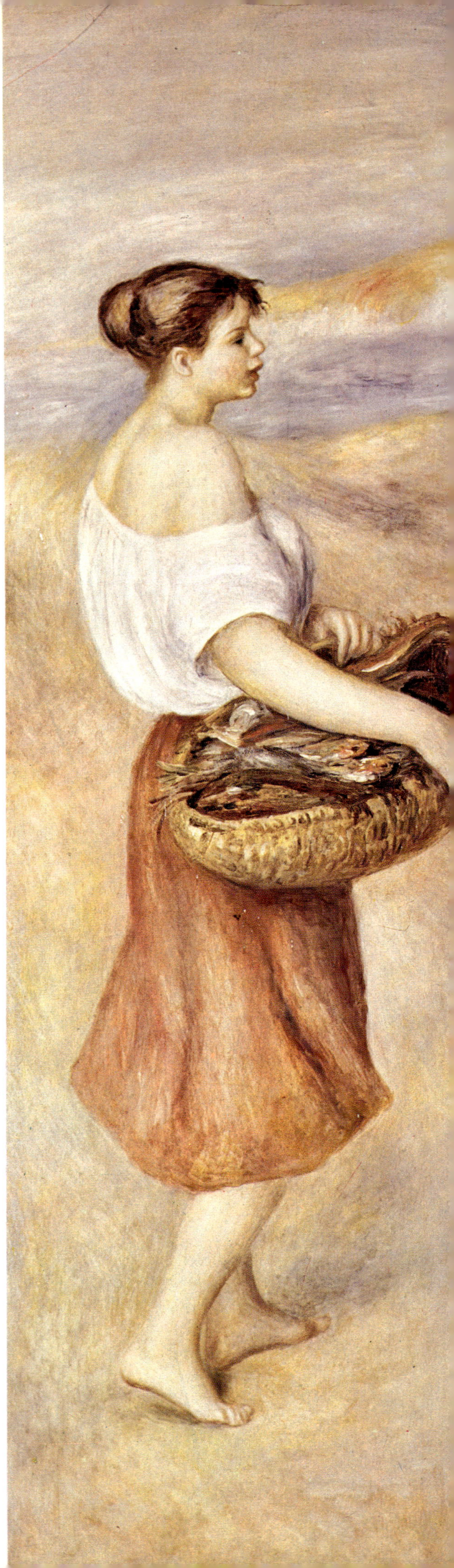

21. *The Fish Vendor* – c. 1889. National Gallery of Art, Washington, D.C.

22. *Sketch for "The Large Bathers"* – 1884-1885. M. Paul Pétridès Collection, Paris

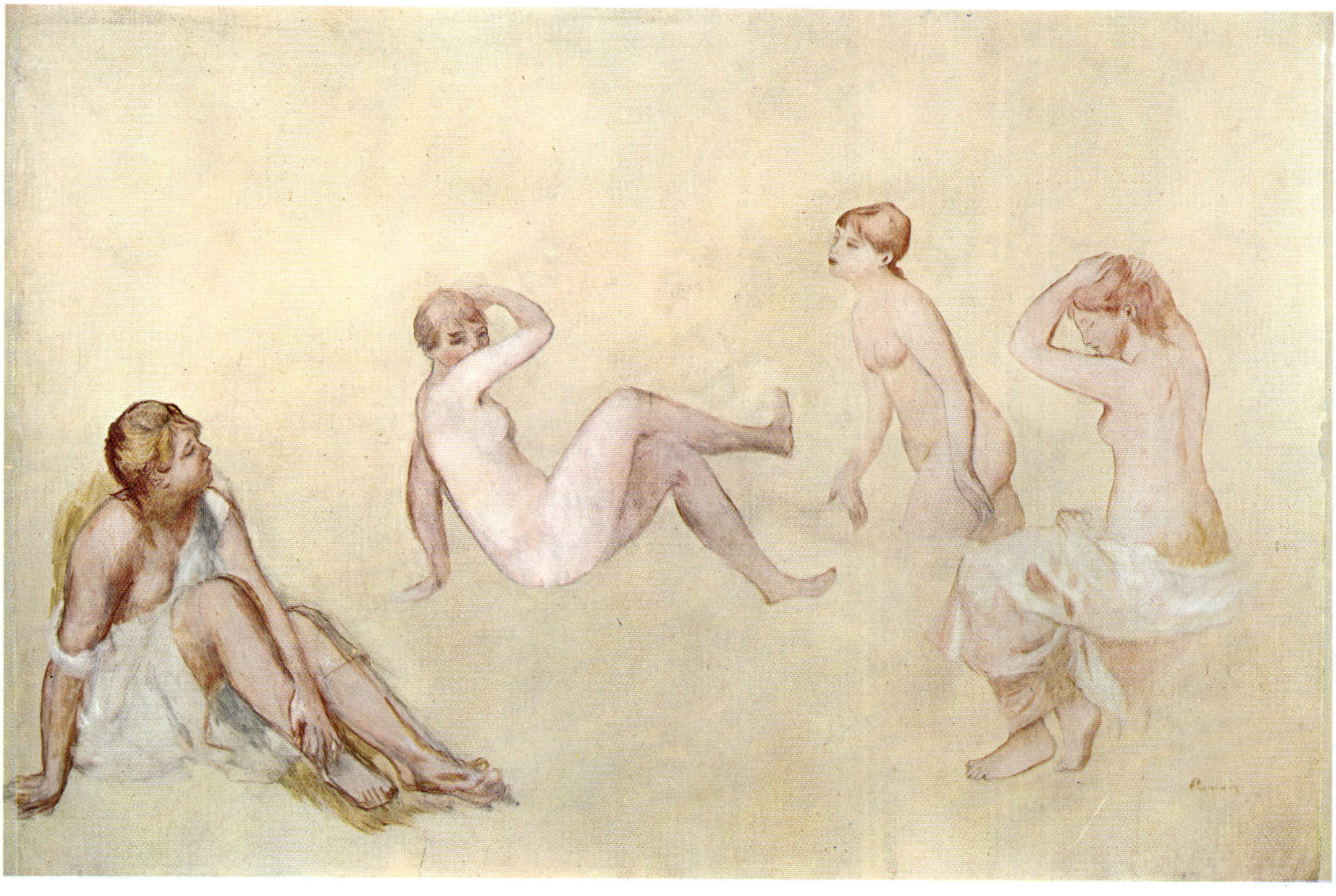

23. *The Large Bathers* – 1887. Mrs C.S. Tyson Collection, Philadelphia

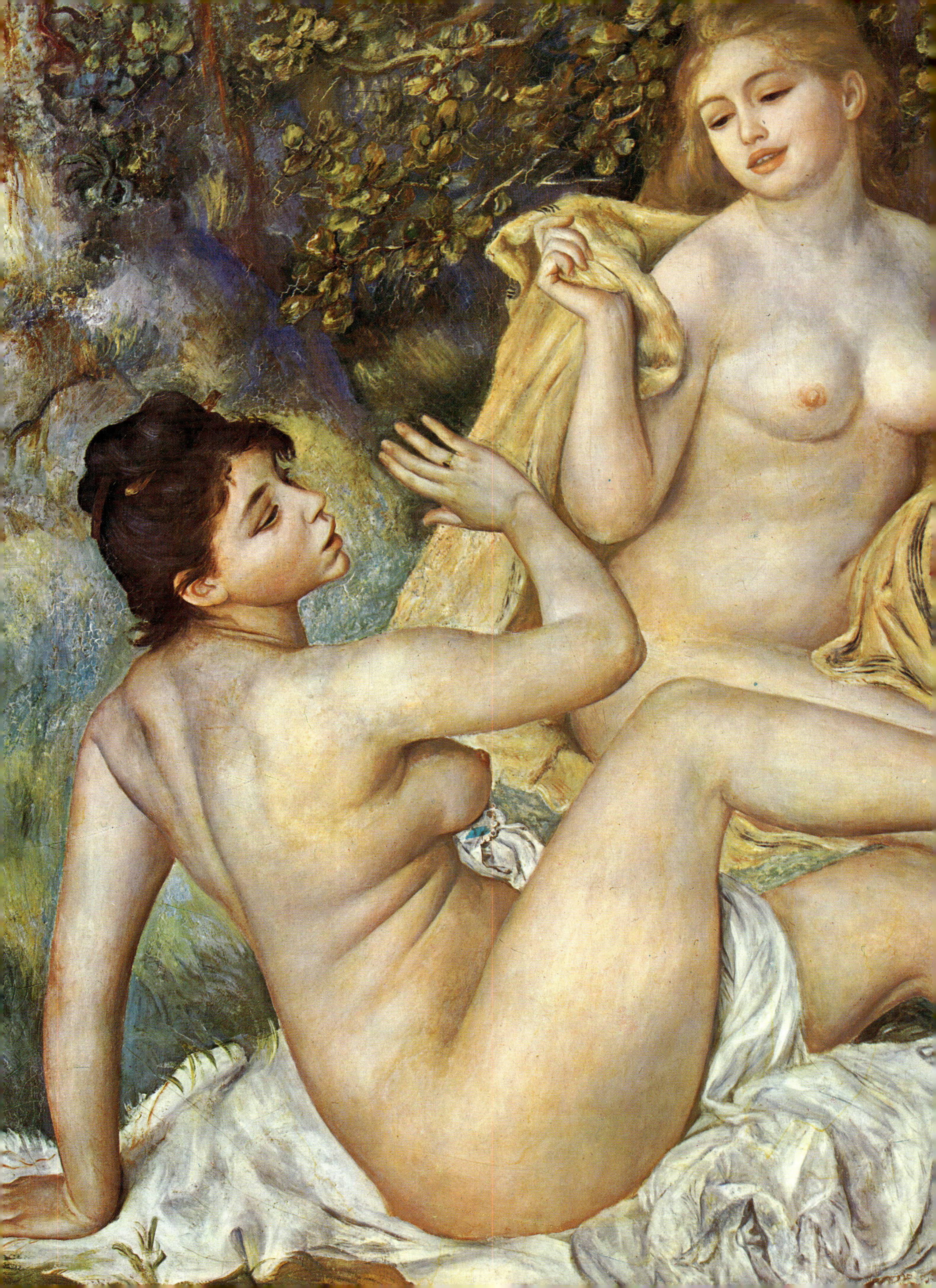

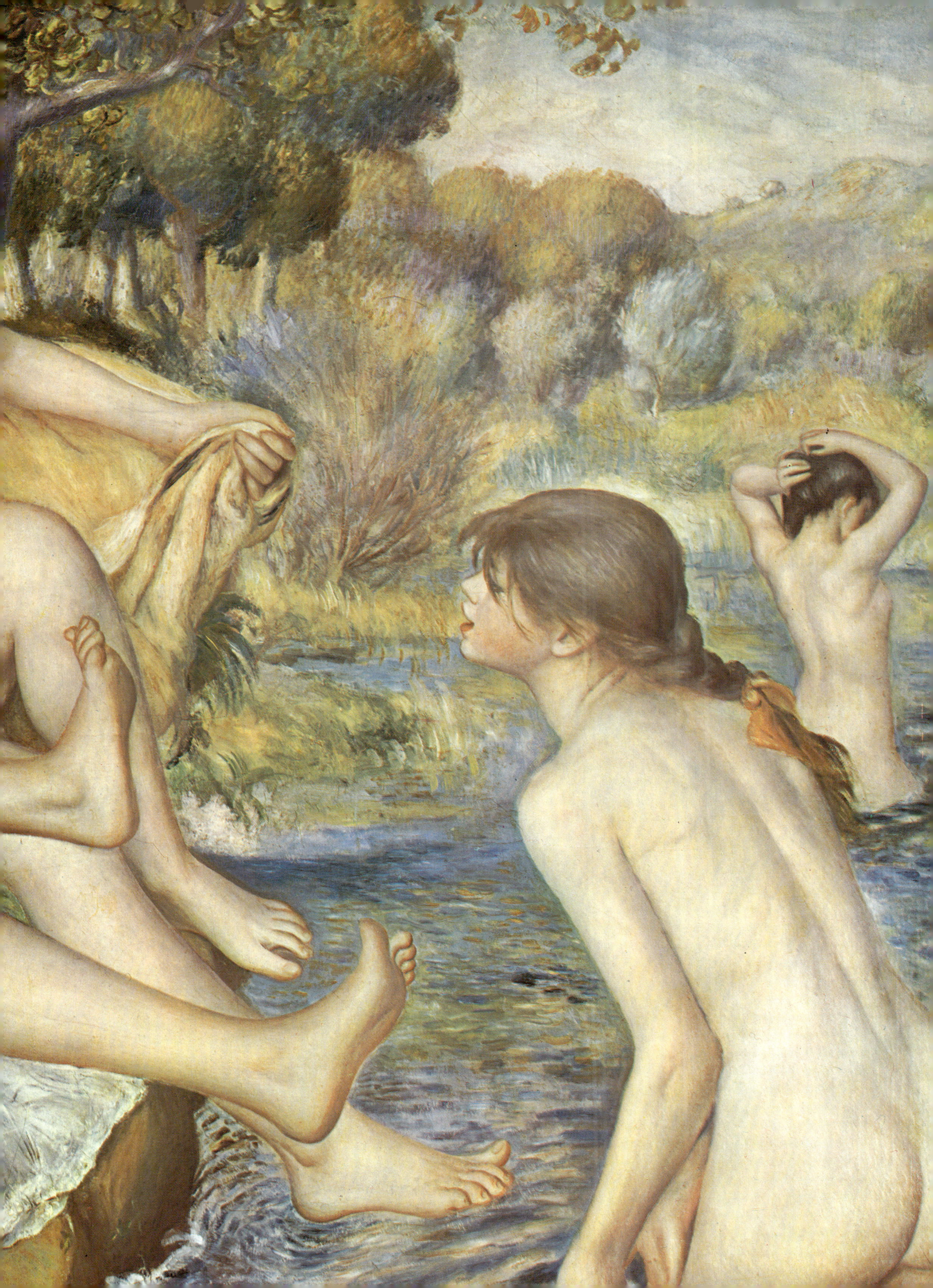

24. *Motherhood, or Woman Nursing Her Child* – 1886. Private collection, New York

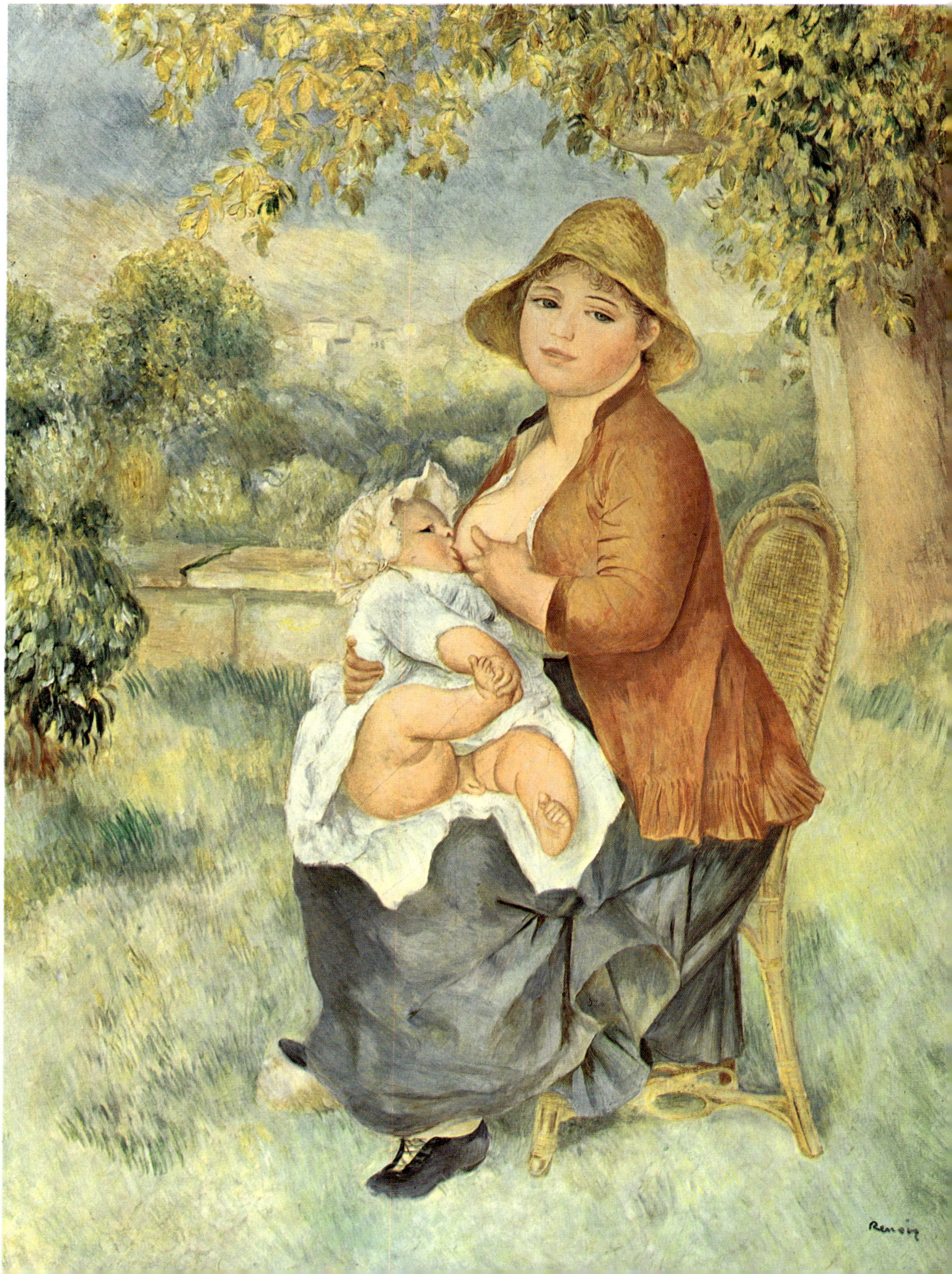

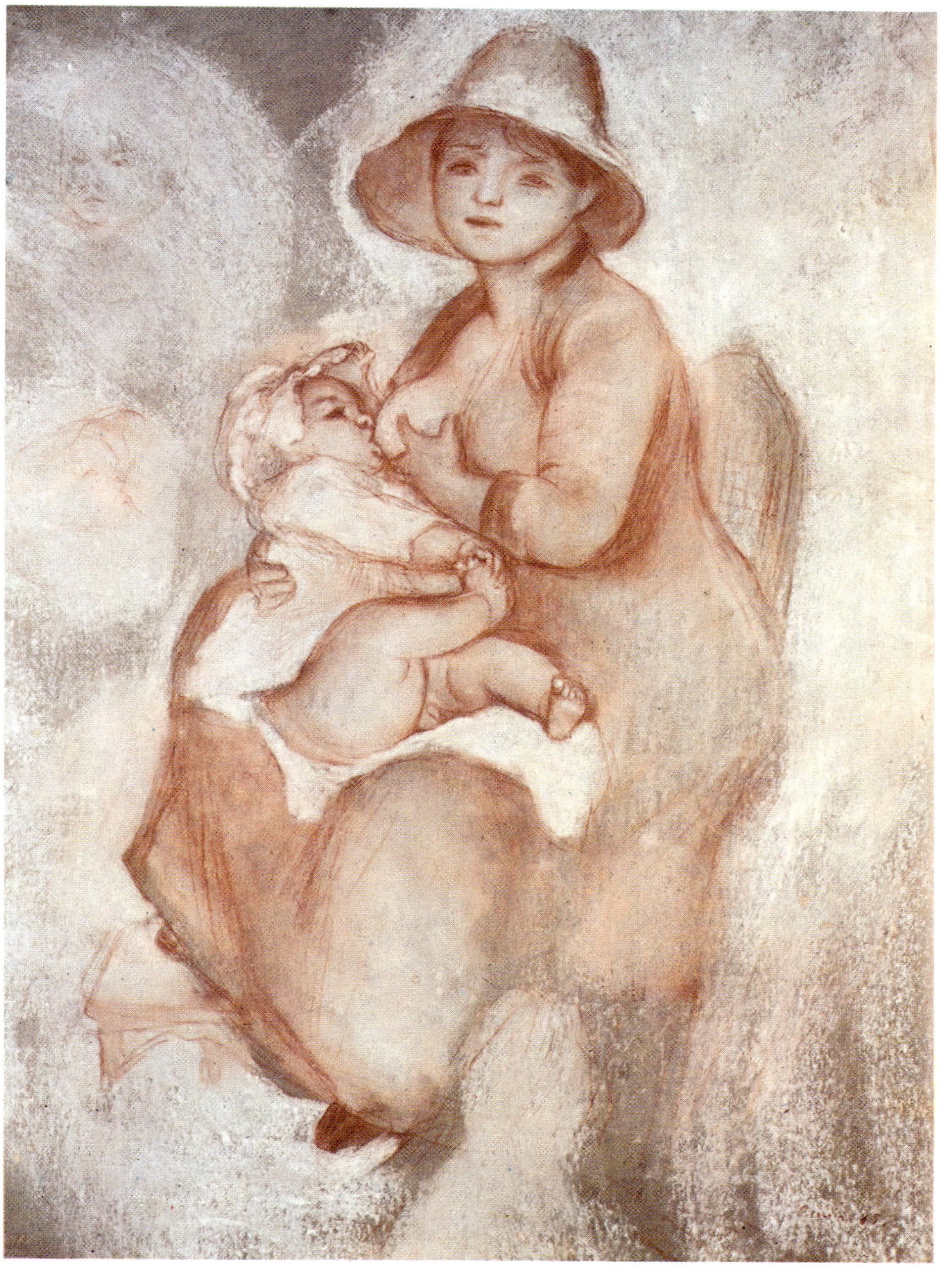

25. *Motherhood* – 1885. Private collection, London

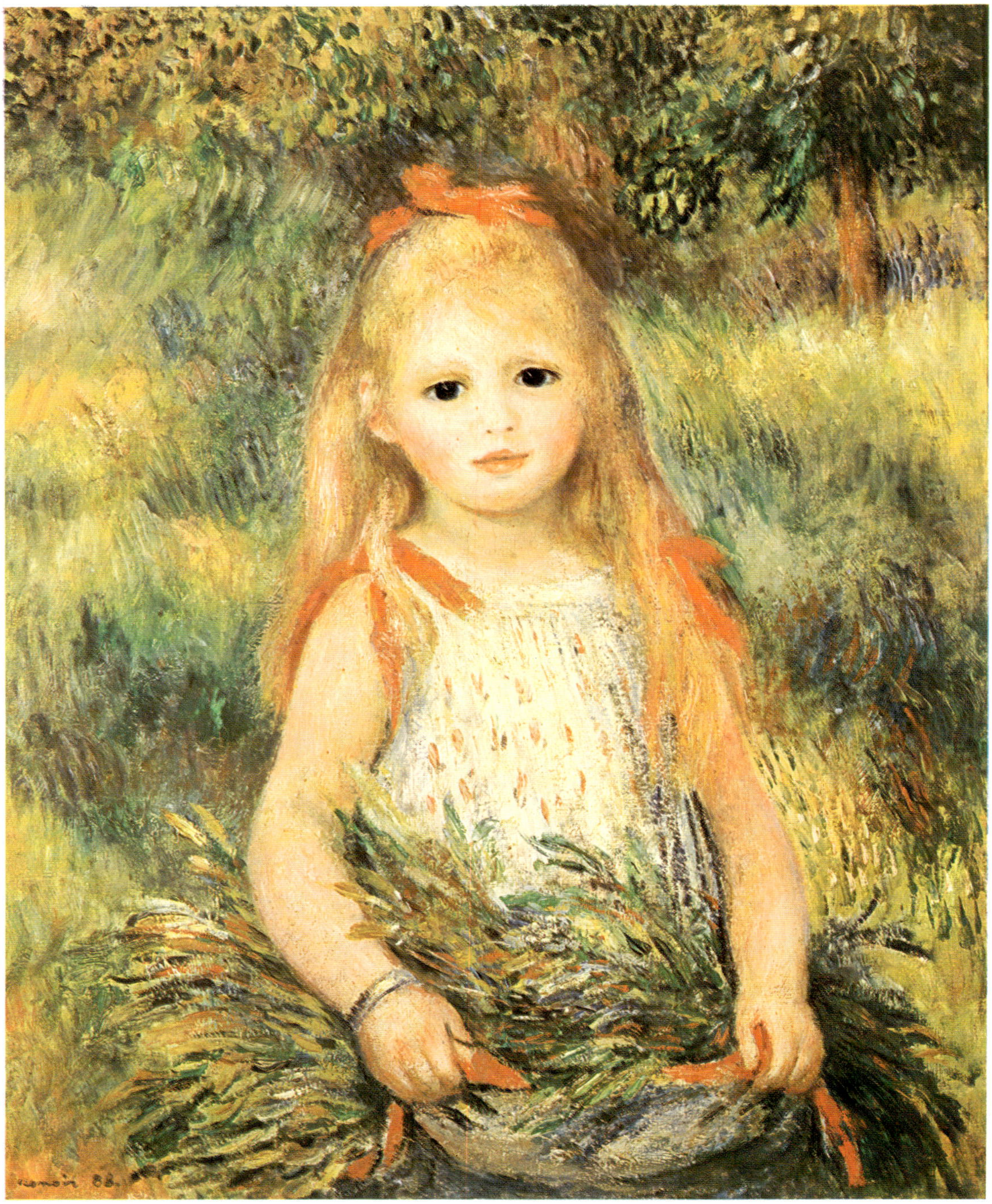

26. *Little Girl with Sheaf of Grass and Wildflowers* – 1888. Museu de Arte, Sâo Paulo

27. *The Daughters of Catulle Mendès* – 1888. The Hon. and Mrs Walter H. Annenberg Collection, London

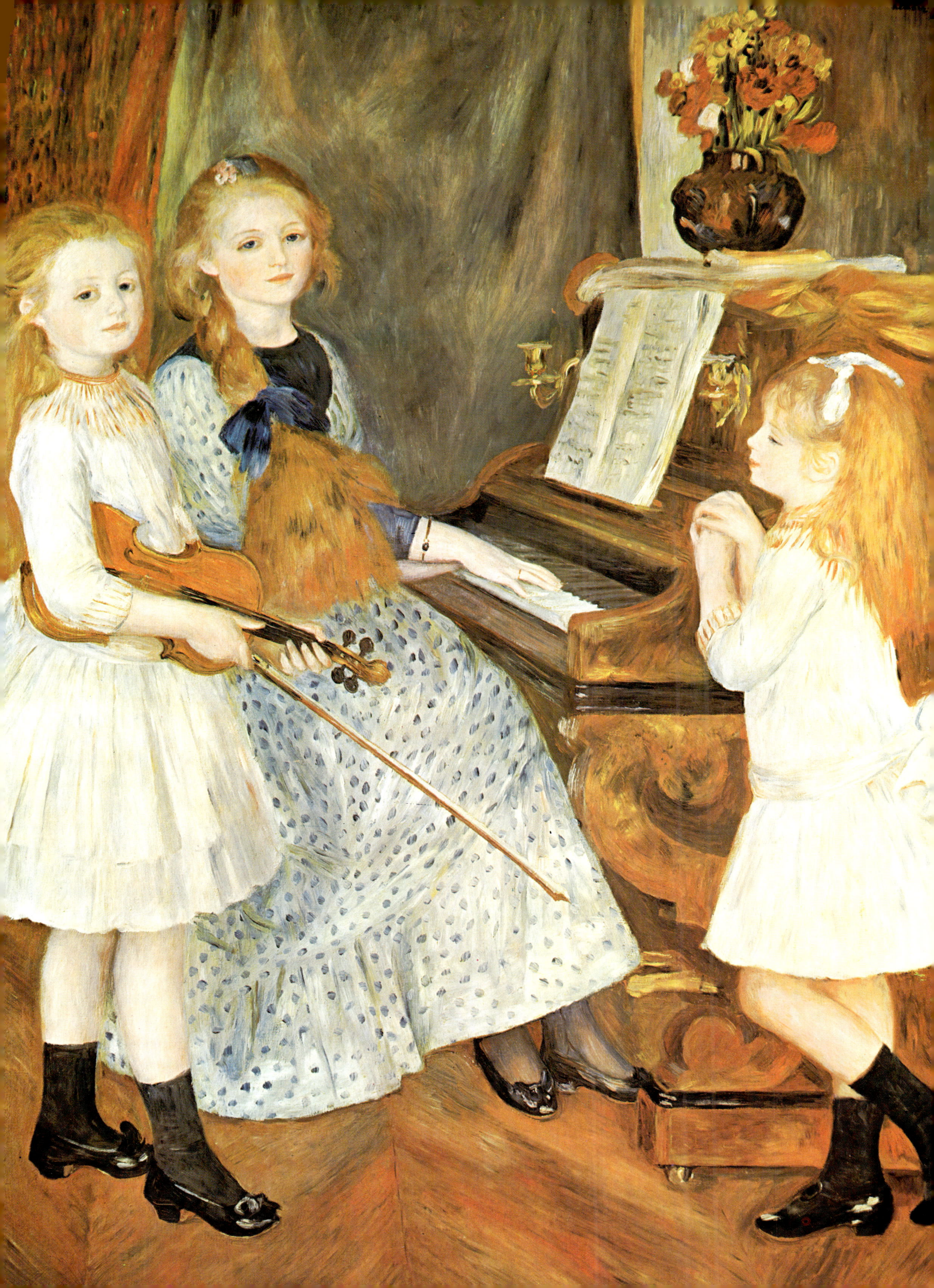

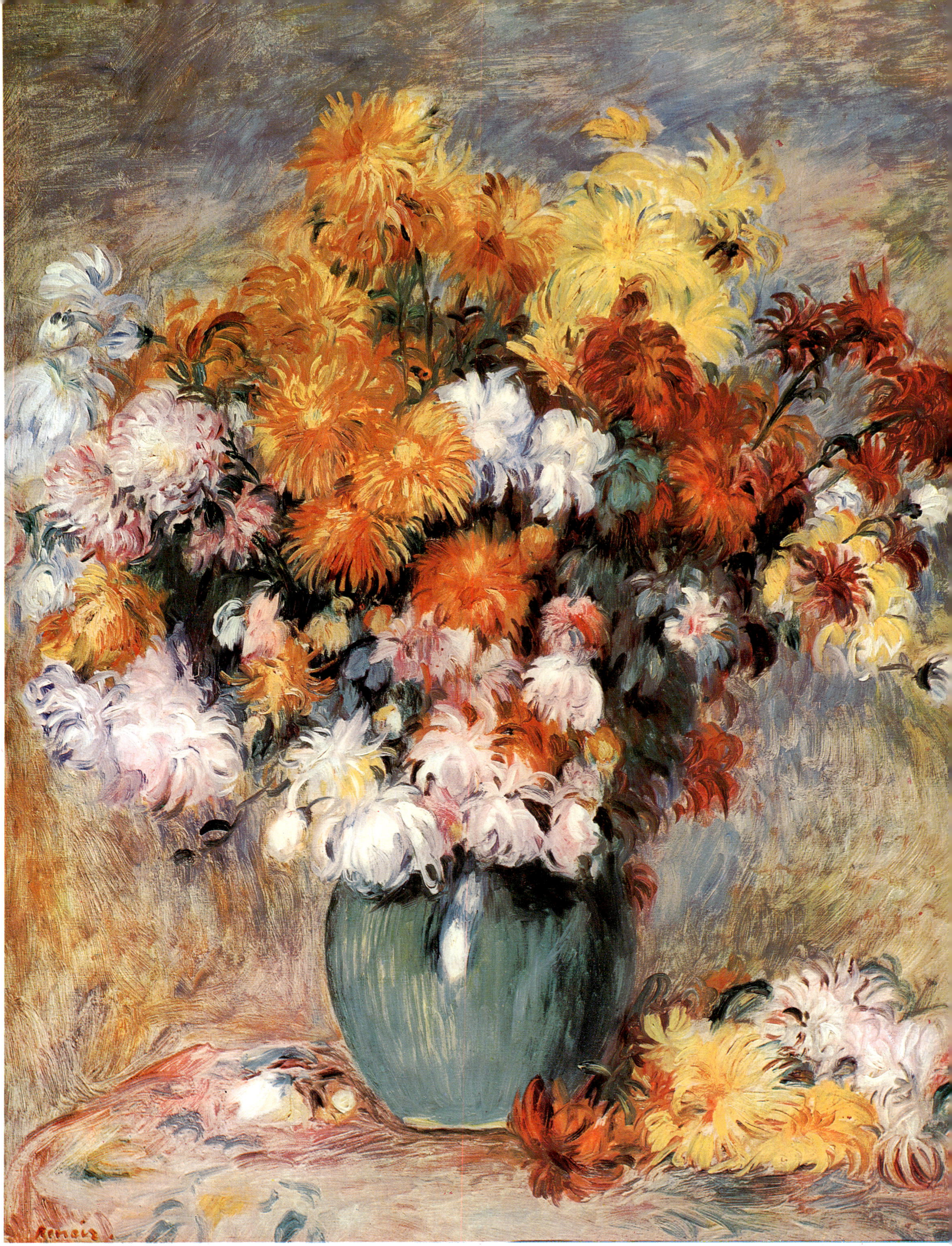

28. *Vase of Chrysanthemums* – Musée des Beaux-Arts, Rouen

29. *The Apple Vendor* – 1890. Cleveland Museum (Leonard C. Hanna Jr. Collection), Cleveland

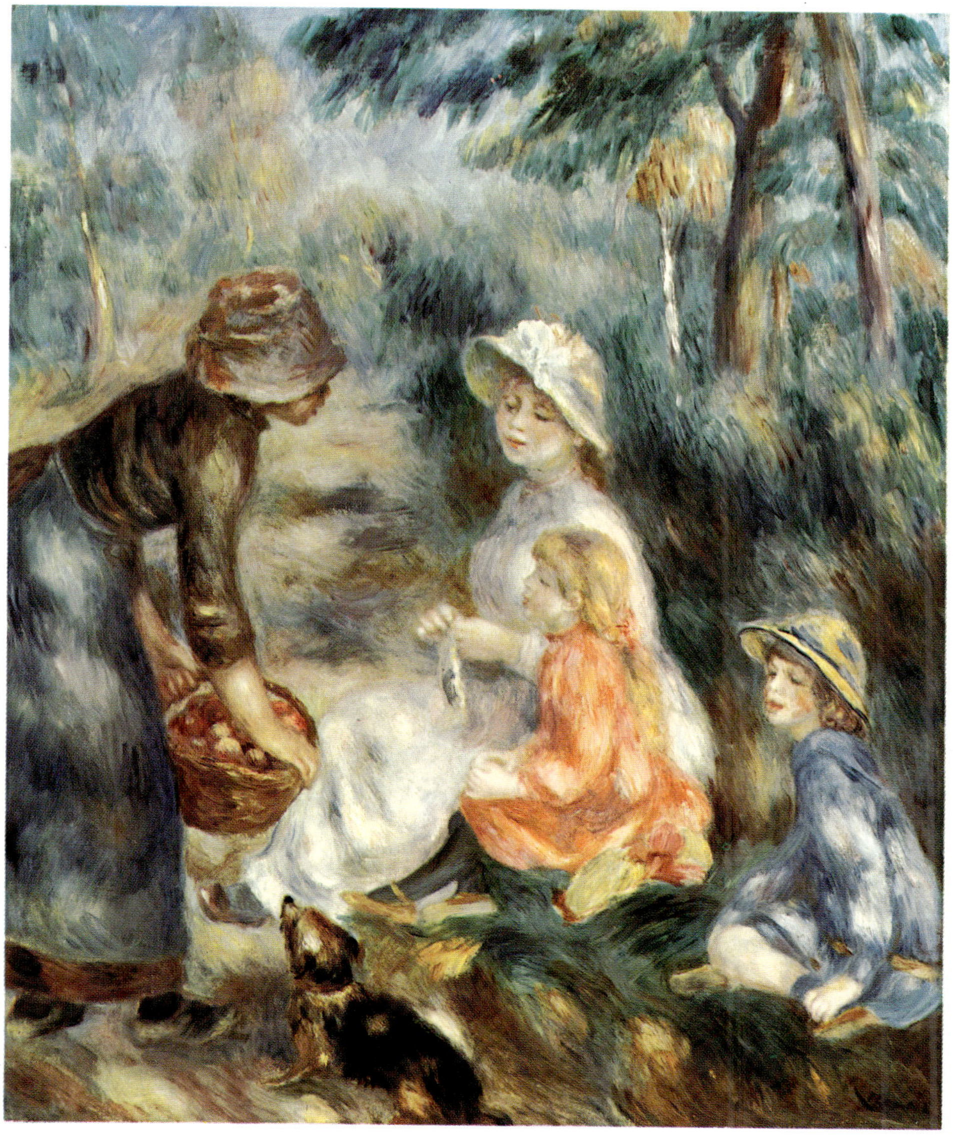

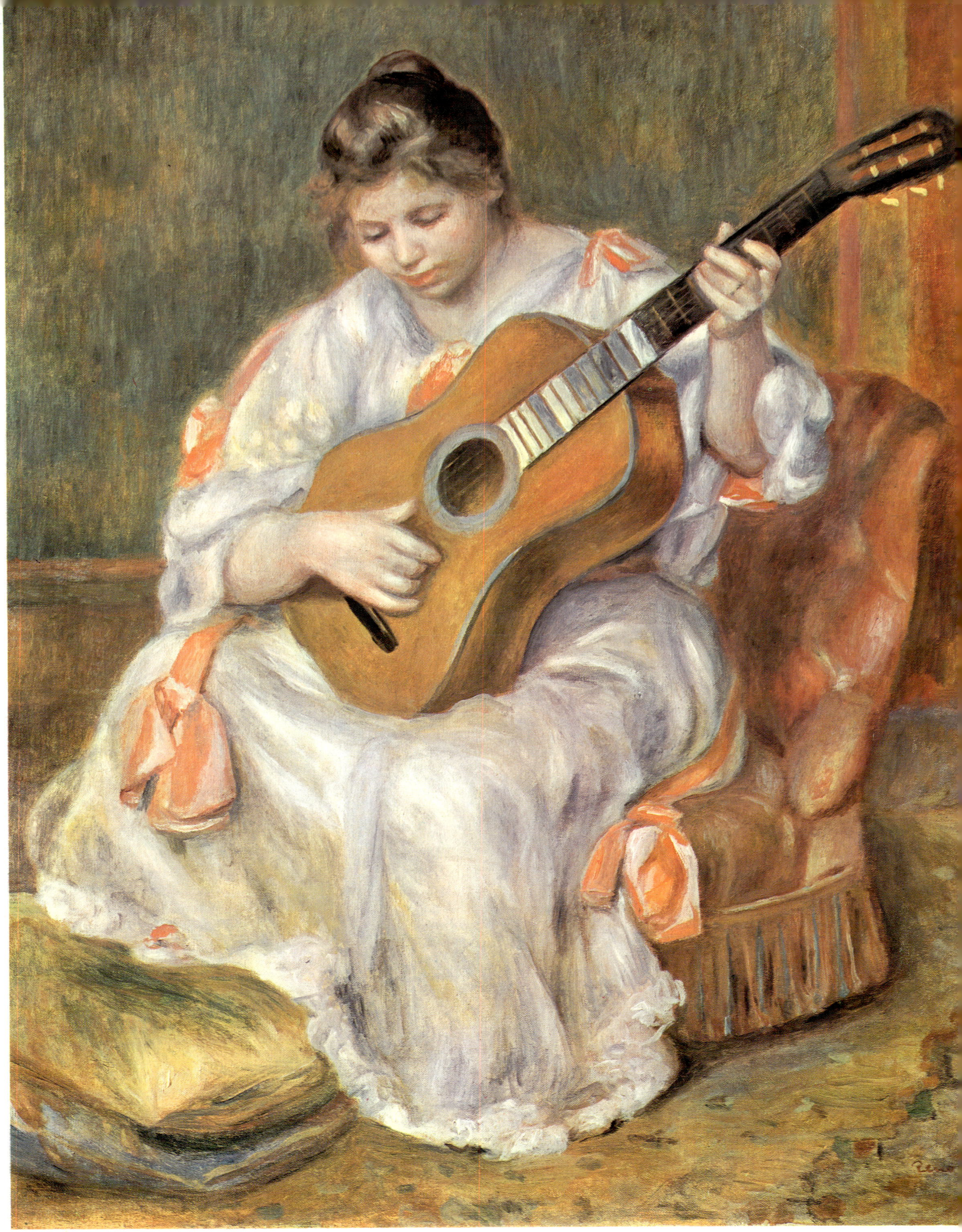

30. *Woman Playing the Guitar* – Musée des Beaux-Arts, Lyons

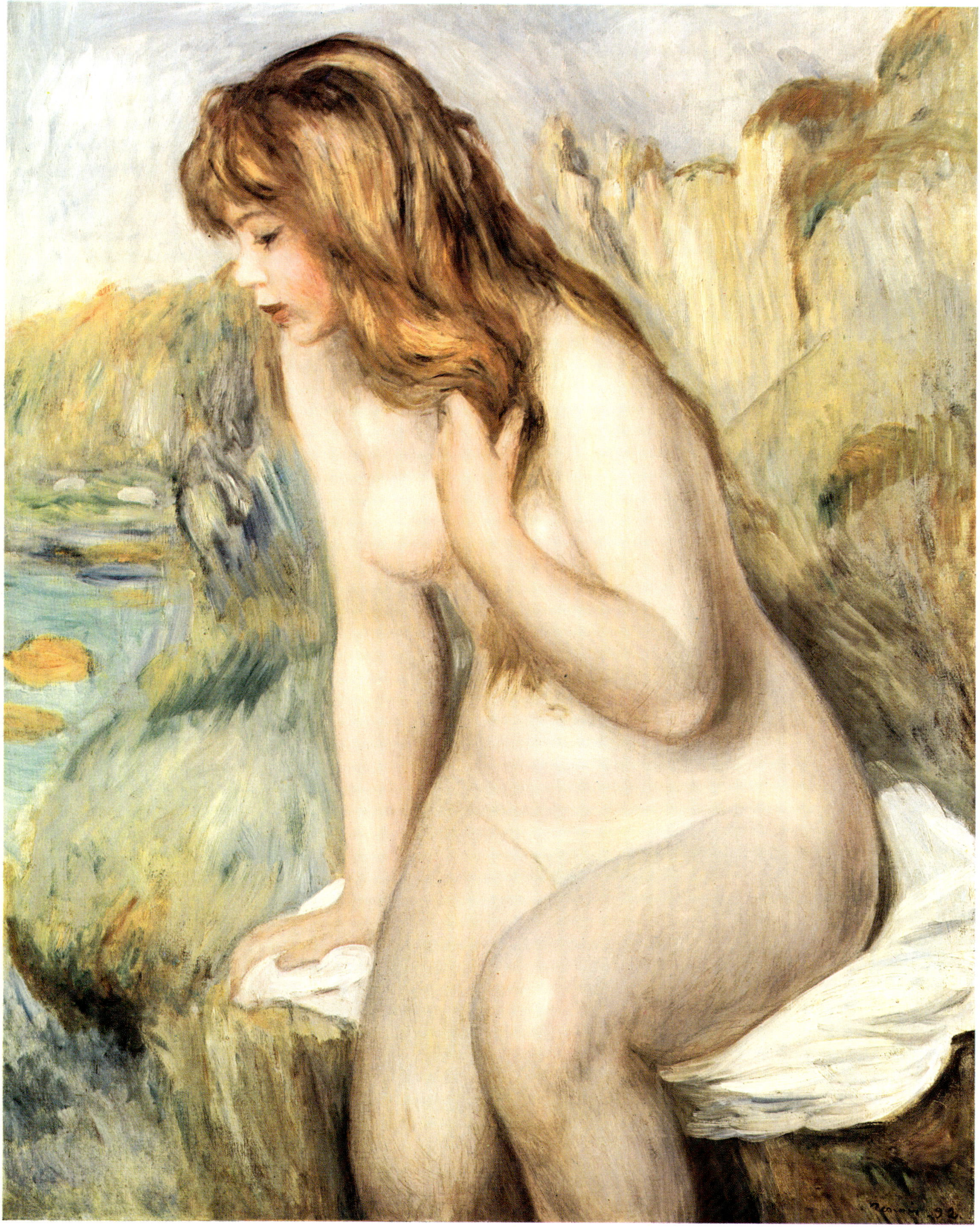

31. *Bather Sitting on a Rock* – 1892. Private collection, Paris

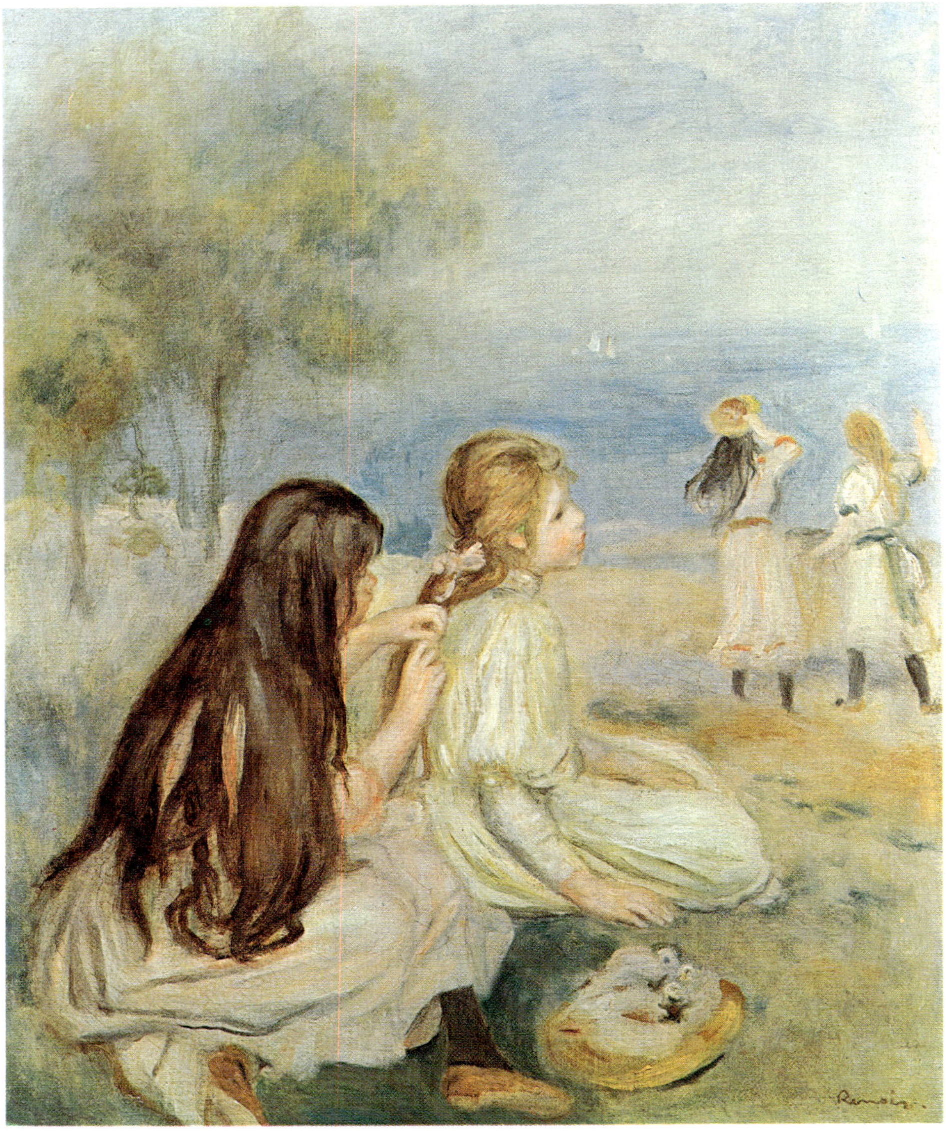

32. *Girls by the Seaside* – 1894. Baron Louis de Chollet Collection, Fribourg (Switzerland)

33. *In the Meadow, or Gathering Flowers* – 1890. Metropolitan Museum of Art, New York

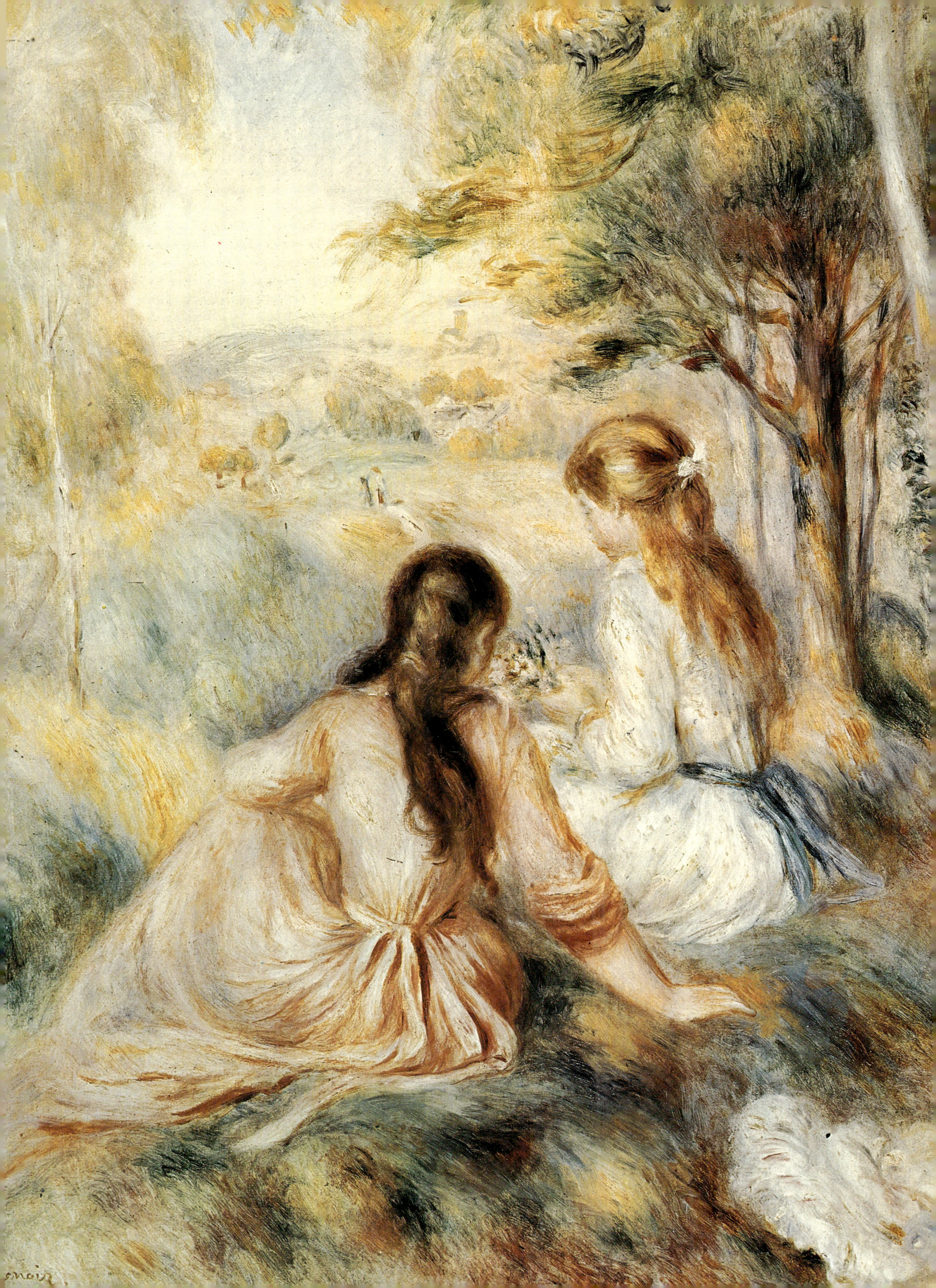

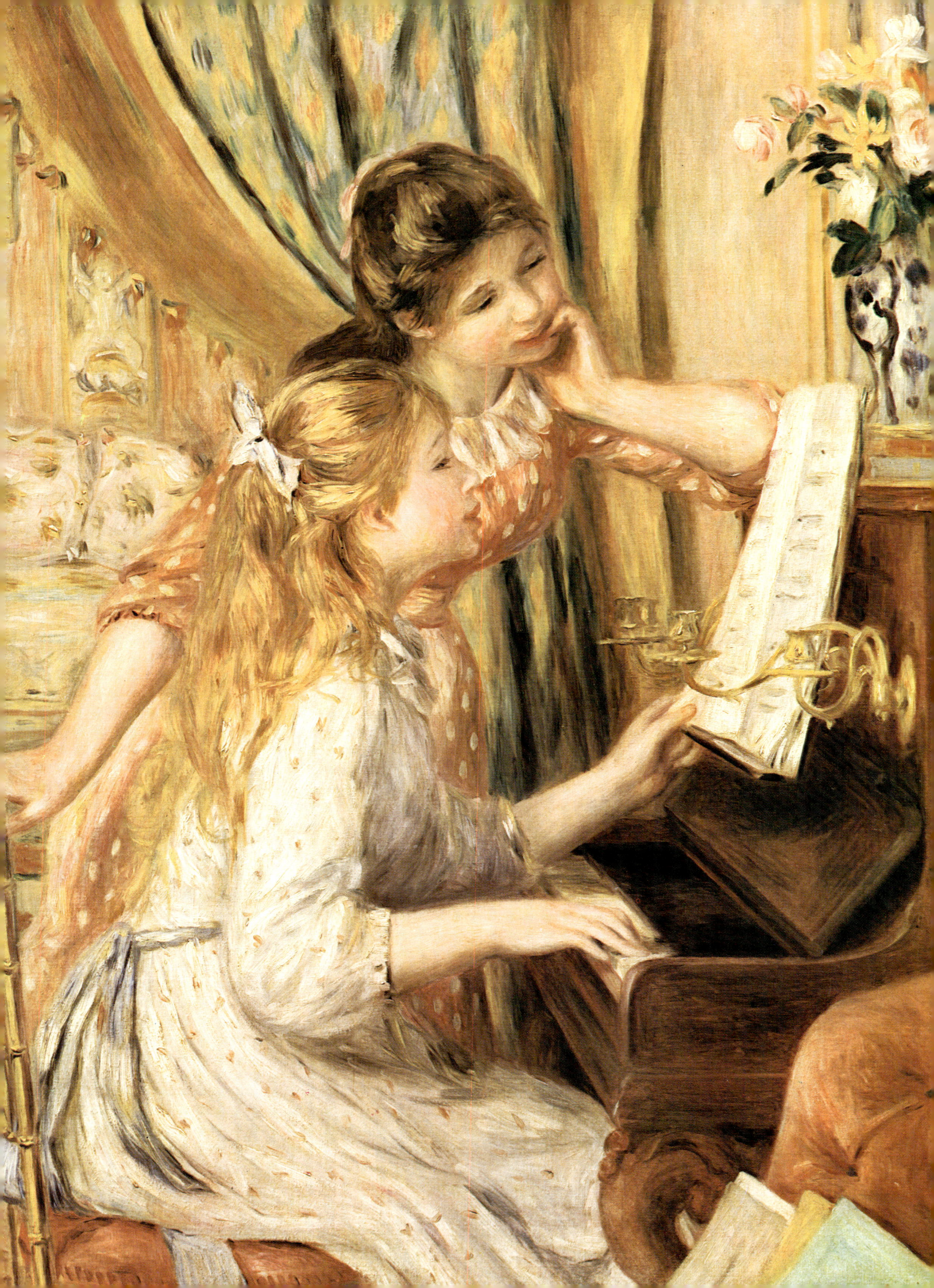

34. *At the Piano* – 1892. Musée d'Orsay, Paris

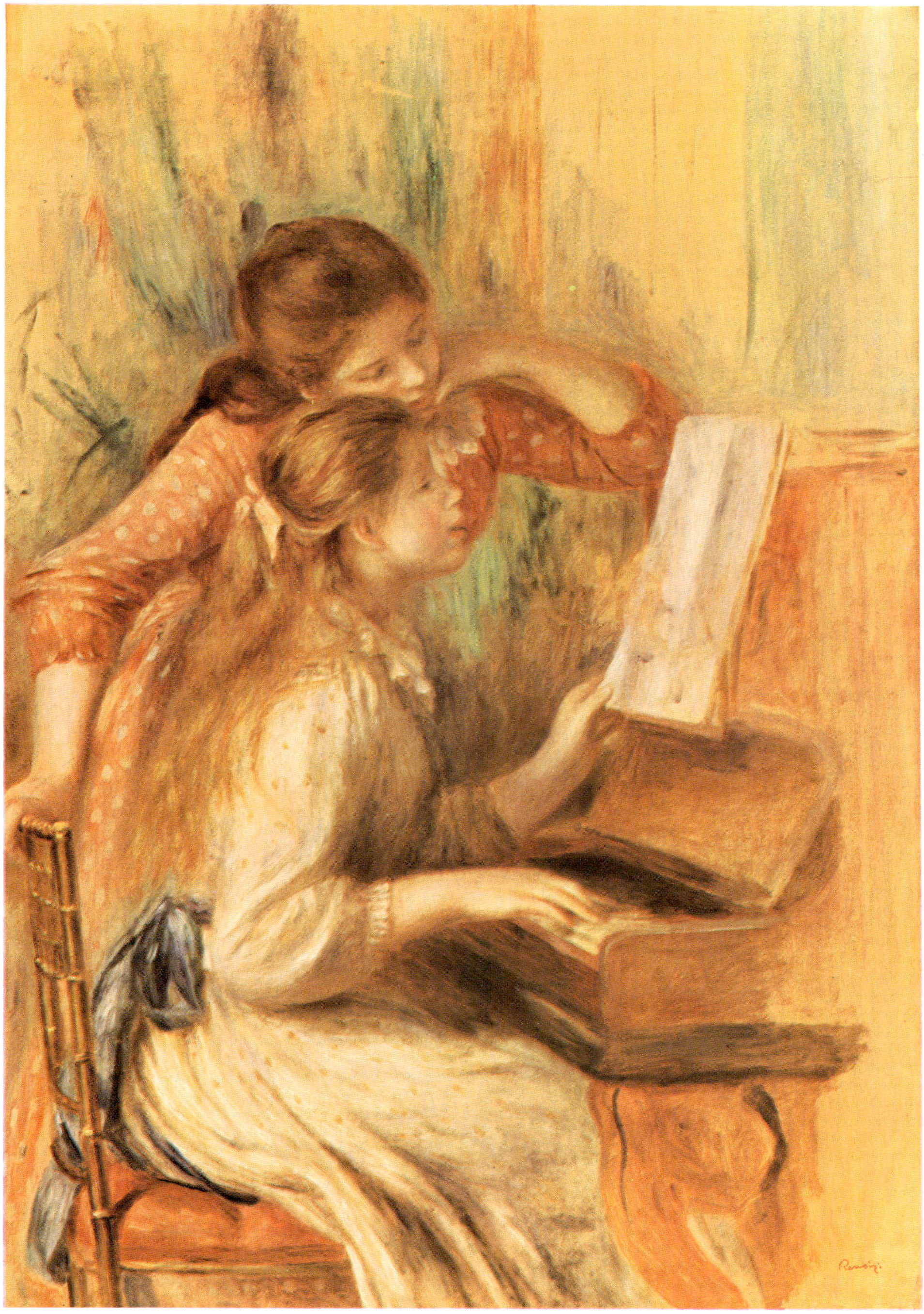

35. *At the Piano* – 1892. Madame Jean Walter Collection, Paris

36. *Still-Life with Cup and Sugar Bowl* – 1904. Private collection, Paris

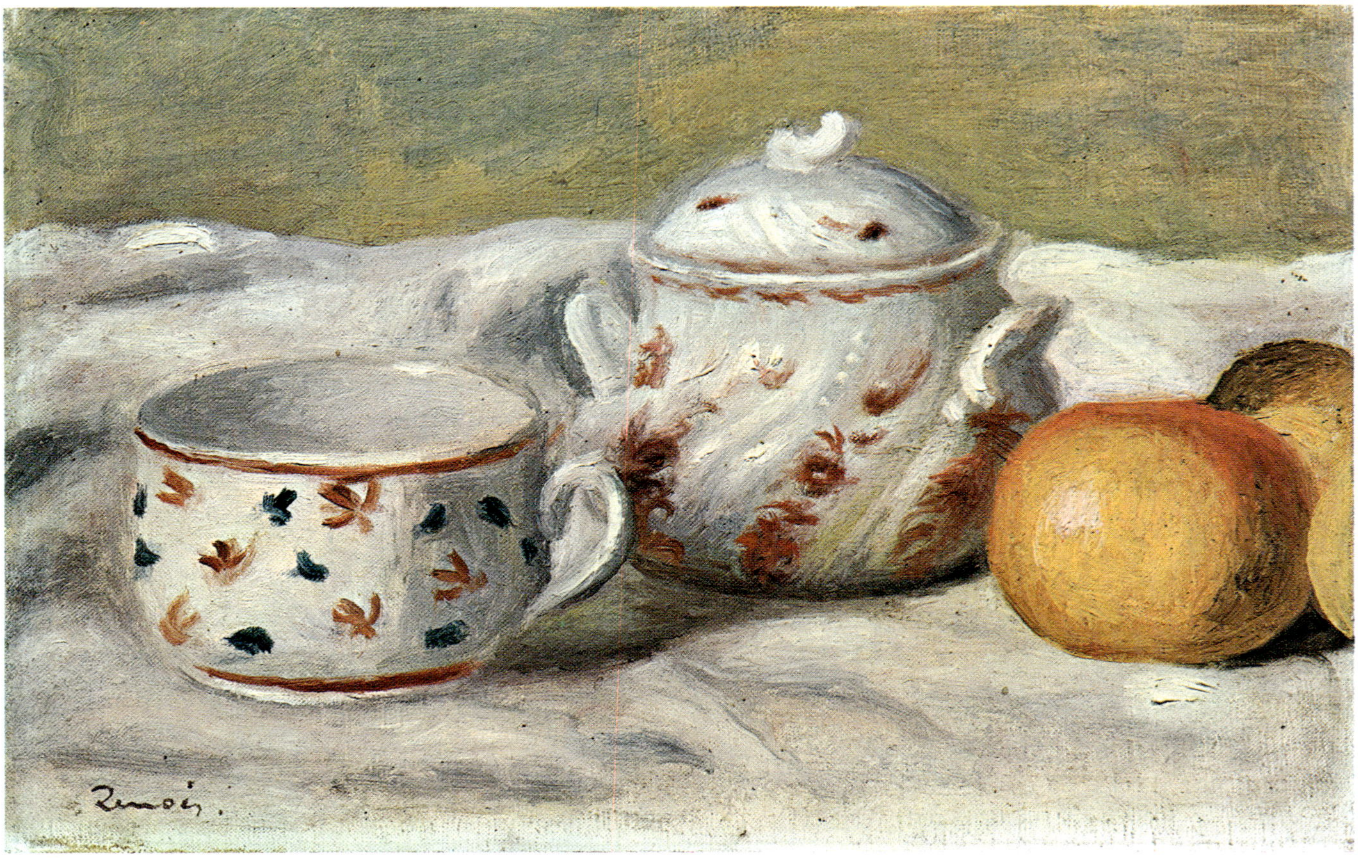

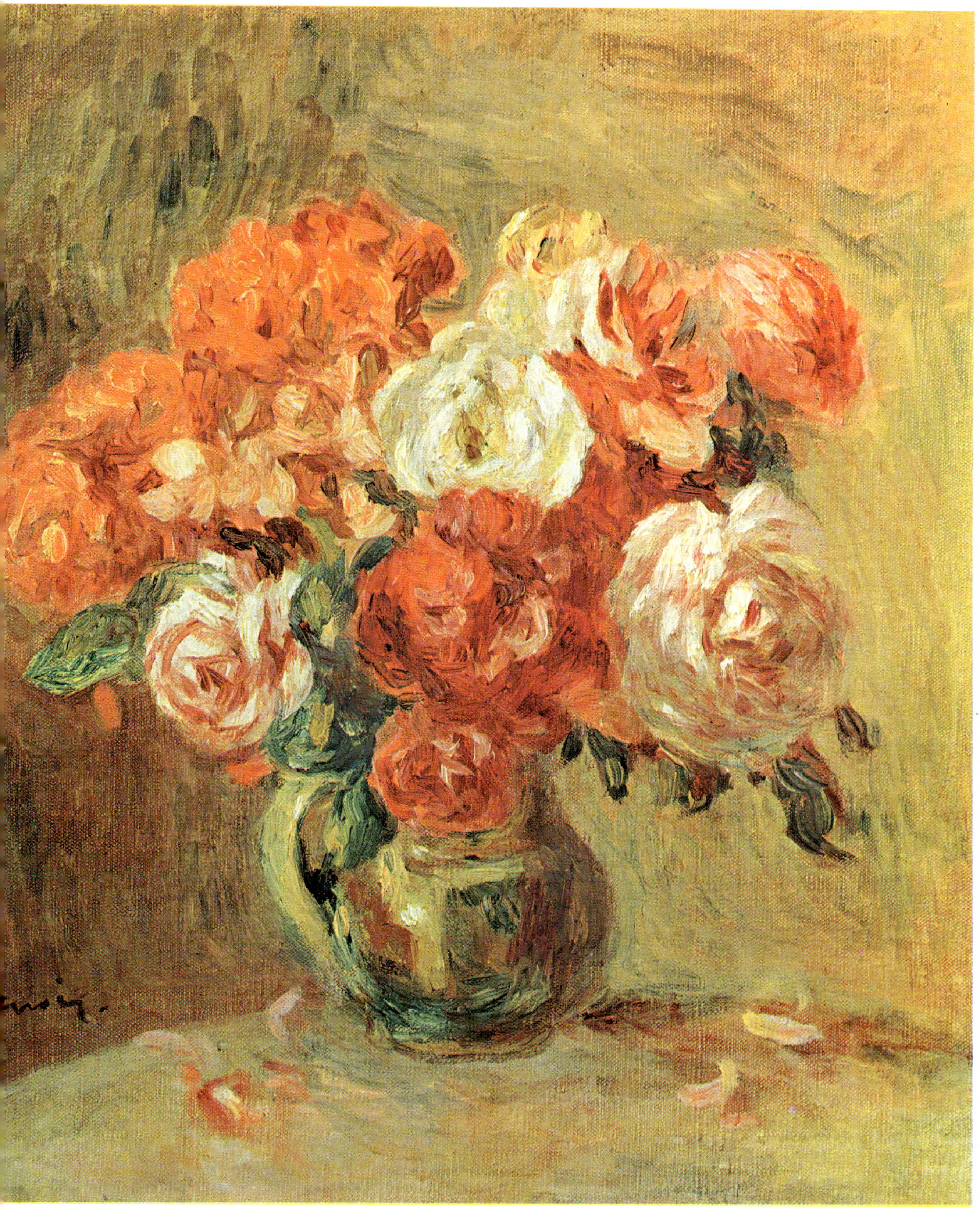

37. *Flowers in a Vase* – 1901. Private collection, Ireland

38. *Cros-de-Cagnes* – 1905. Private collection, Lausanne

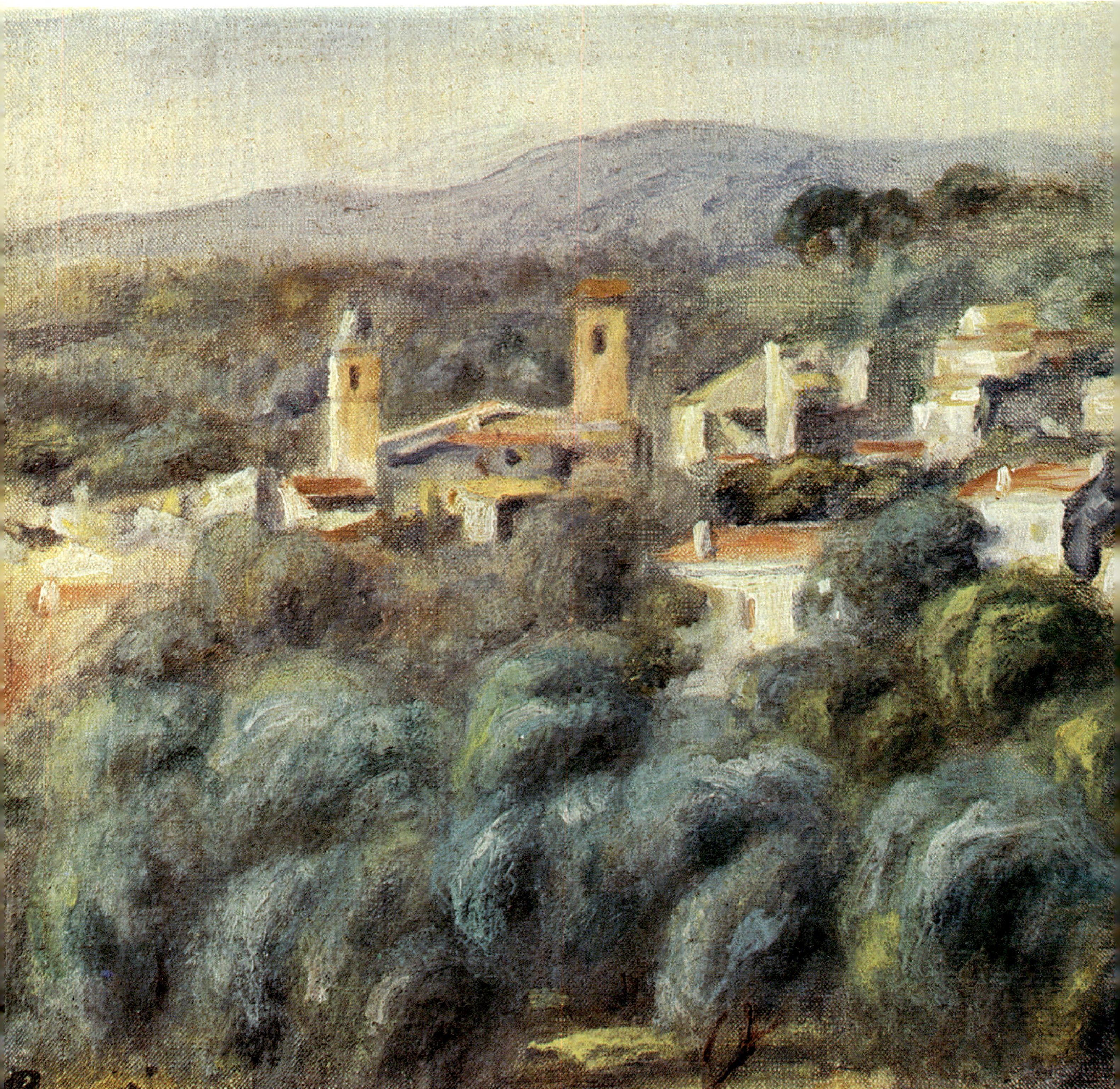

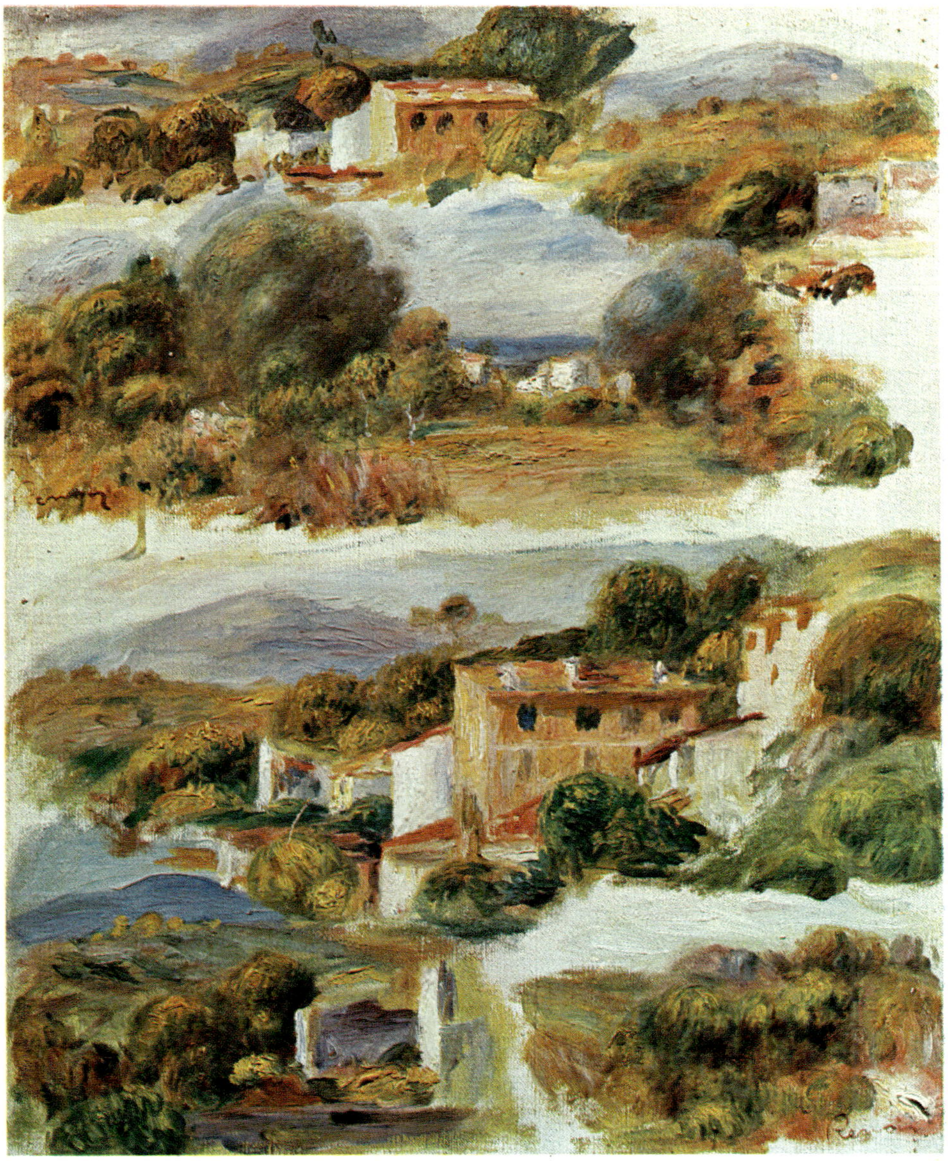

39. *Houses at Cagnes* – 1905. Private collection, Paris

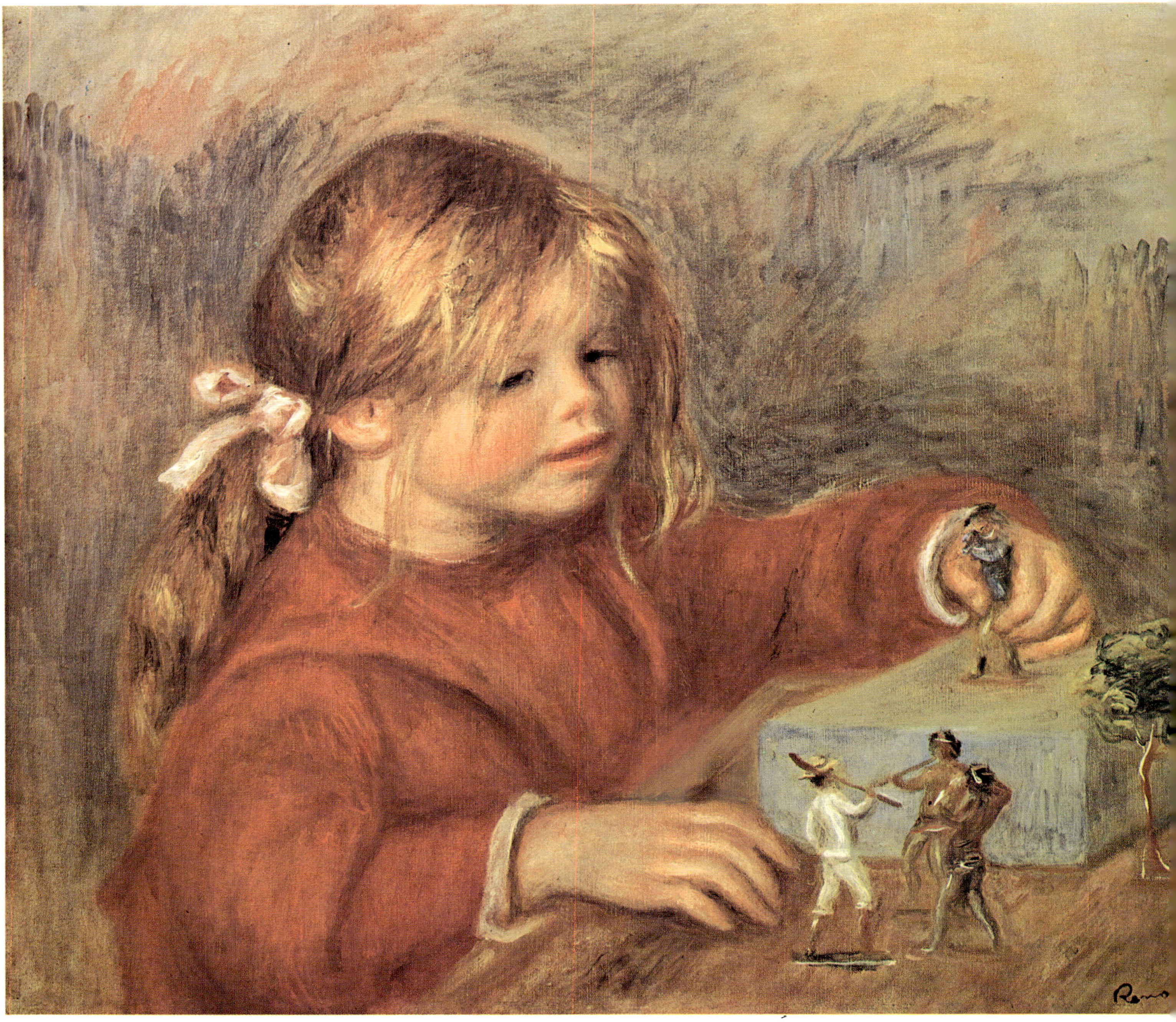

40. *Claude Renoir Playing with His Toys* – c. 1906. Madame Jean Walter Collection, Paris

41. *Self-Portrait with a White Hat* – 1910. Durand-Ruel Collection, Paris

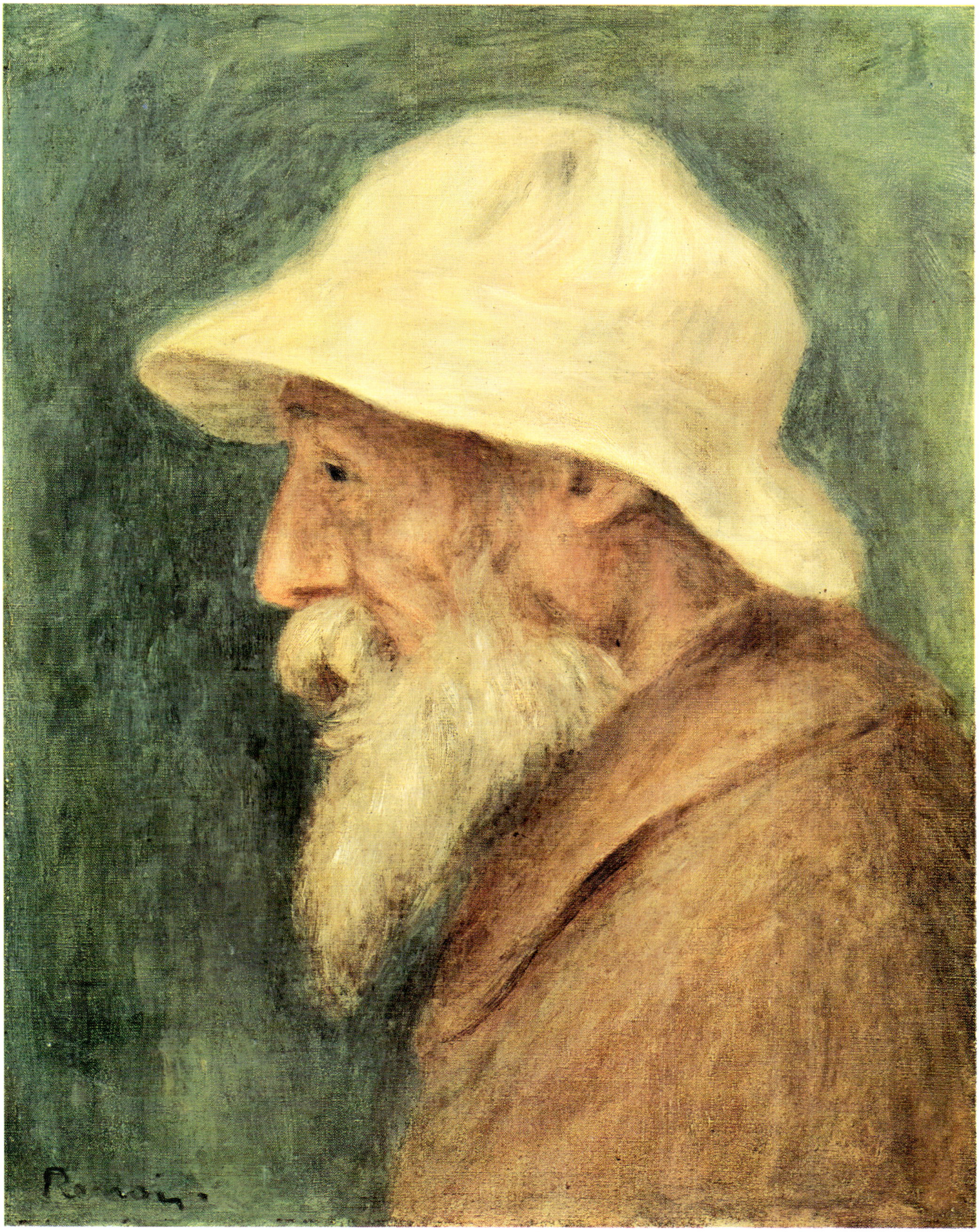

42. *Seated Bather* – 1914. Art Institute, Chicago

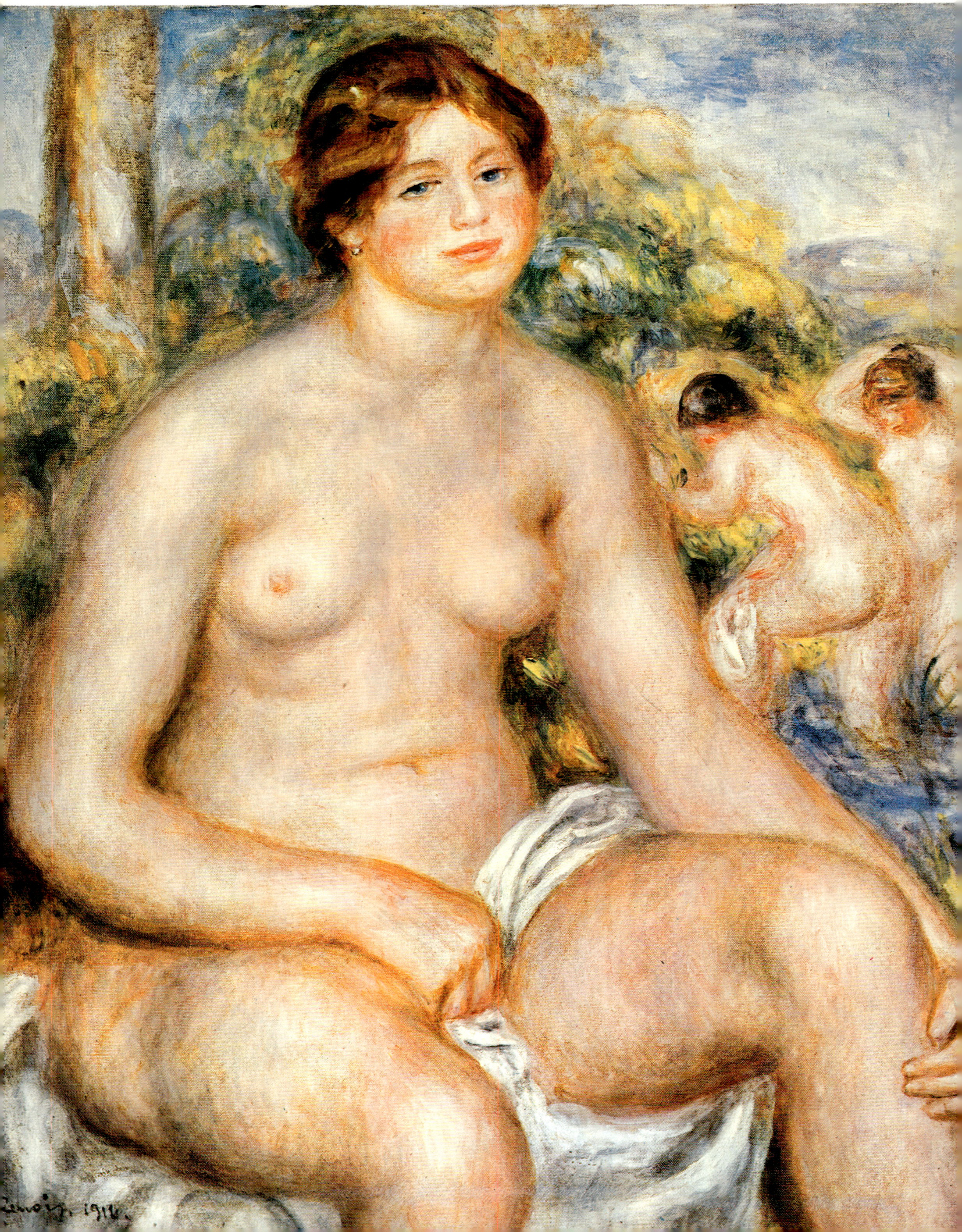

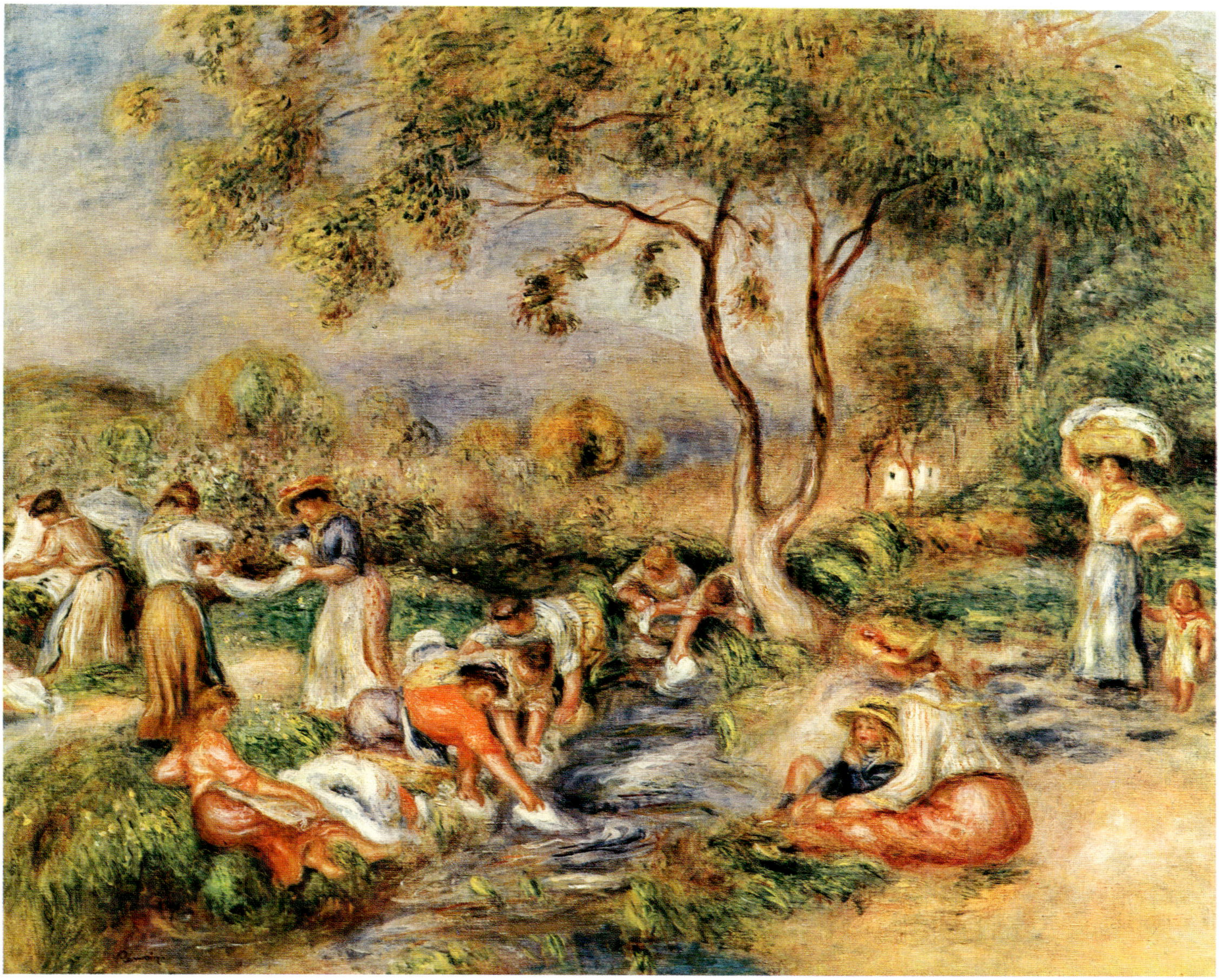

43. *Washerwomen at Cagnes* – 1912. Private collection, Paris

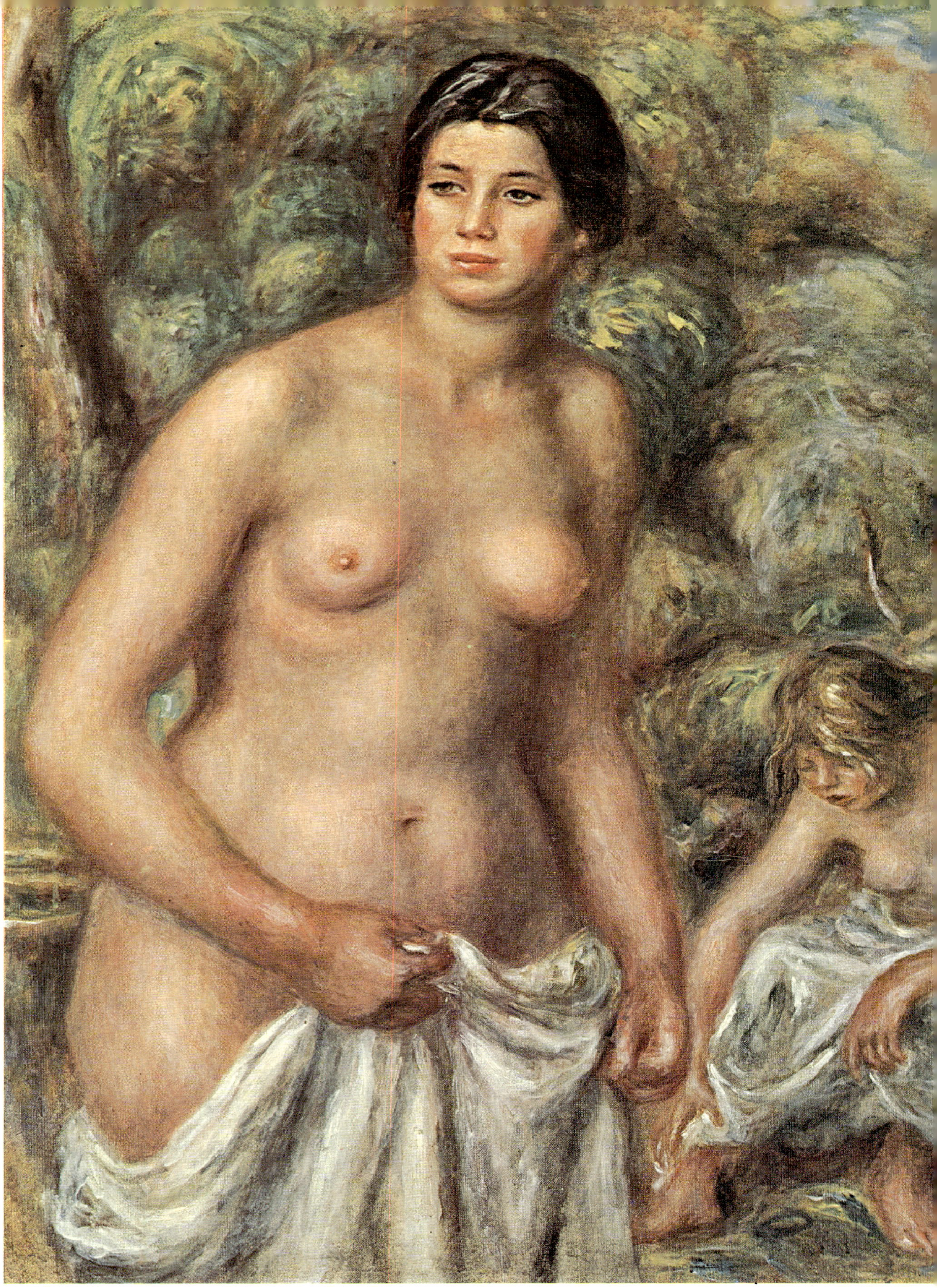

44. *Madeleine Bruno, or The Two Bathers* – 1916. Private collection, Paris

45. *Promenade along the Sea* – Museum of Modern Art (Grassi Collection), Milan

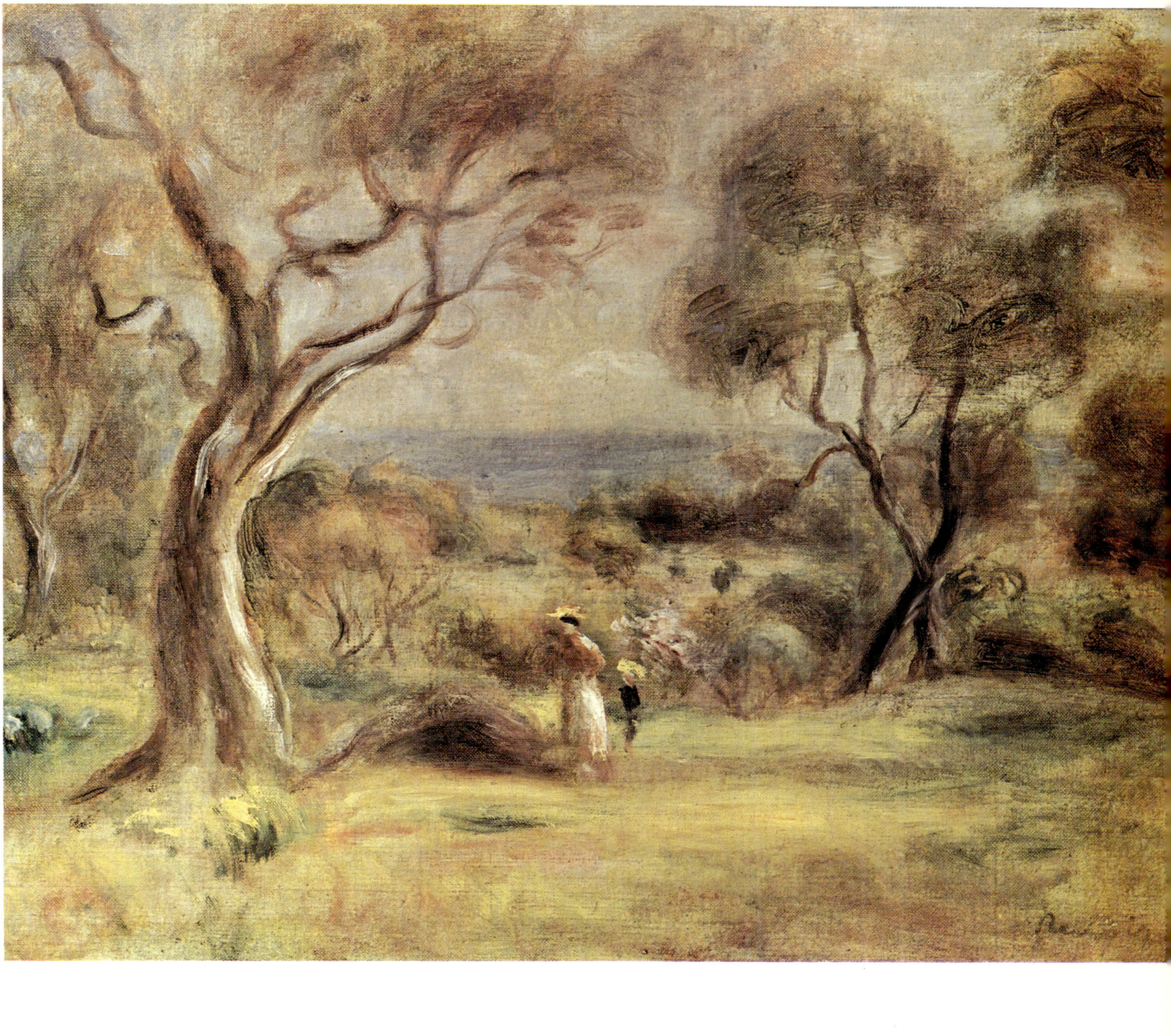

Editor in chief Anna Maria Mascheroni

Art director Luciano Raimondi

Text Deanna Bernar

Translation Terry Rogers

Productiòn DIMA & B, Milan

Photo Credits Gruppo Editoriale Fabbri S.p.A., Milan

Copyright © 1988 by Gruppo Editoriale Fabbri S.p.A., Milan

Copyright © 1990 by PHIDAL
for the Canadian edition

ISBN 2-89393-040-9

Printed in Italy by Gruppo Editoriale Fabbri S.p.A., Milan